**Geoff Tibballs** has written over a hundred books, including such humour titles as *The Mammoth Book of Jokes*, *The Mammoth Book of Comic Quotes* and *The Mammoth Book of Insults*. He feels qualified to write this book as he has just reached the age where he becomes eligible for his free bus pass and his family says he talks sh*t all the time.

# CRAZY SH*T OLD PEOPLE SAY

## Geoff Tibballs

Constable • London

Constable & Robinson Ltd

3 The Lanchesters
162 Fulham Palace Road
London W6 9ER

www.constablerobinson.com

First published in the UK by Constable,
an imprint of Constable & Robinson Ltd., 2011

Copyright © Geoff Tibballs 2011

The right of Geoff Tibballs to be identified as the author of this
work has been asserted by him in accordance with the
Copyright, Designs and Patents Act 1988

A copy of the British Library Cataloguing in
Publication data is available from the British Library

UK ISBN 978-1-84901-715-2

3 5 7 9 10 8 6 4 2

First published in the United States in 2011 by Running Press Book Publishers

9 8 7 6 5 4 3 2

Digit on the right indicates the number of this printing

US Library of Congress Control Number 2011923059
US ISBN 978-0-7624-4236-2

Running Press Book Publishers
2300 Chestnut Street
Philadelphia, PA 19103-4371

Visit us on the web!

www.runningpress.com

Printed and bound in the UK

# Contents

# Introduction

With old age comes grey hair, dodgy knees, a sudden passion for reruns of *Murder, She Wrote,* and an apparent God-given licence to speak one's mind and be generally offensive without fear of retribution. Under the guise of passing on the benefits of their experience to family members, or just casual acquaintances, old people exercise their right to swear, cuss and insult as they please. And it's not just old men who turn the air blue. As anyone who has ever tried to stop an aged person pushing into the Post Office queue on pension day will testify, old women can also unleash the sort of language that would make a stand-up comedian blush.

These feisty philosophers take no prisoners as they use their scalpel-like tongues to dissect modern life and the younger generations. They operate under the simple belief that life was much tougher in their day, so young people should just stop moaning and get on with it. "And we had to live it all in black and white!"

If challenged over their outrageous comments, they'll play the age card; you know the sort of thing – "I'm eighty-six, I've fought for my country, and if I want to call you a no good, lowdown, useless fuckwit, then I'll call you a no good, lowdown, useless fuckwit, Vicar."

# 1

# Life's a Bitch: Deal With It

*If you're looking for sympathy from an old person, forget it. It's like getting blood out of a Jehovah's Witness. After all, old people have lived through a world war, rationing, several recessions and over fifty years of the Eurovision Song Contest, so they're not likely to feel sorry for you simply because you've smashed up your new car, your boss is taking you for granted or because the "sexy hot chick" you met on the Internet turned out to be a sixty-five-year-old granny with teeth like a rake.*

"You know where you find sympathy? Right between shit and syphilis in the dictionary!"

"You can wish all you want. You can wish in one hand and crap in the other. See which gets filled first."

"Life's a bitch. Deal with it. Just accept that some days you're the pigeon, some days you're the statue."

"It bugs me when people say, 'Life is short.' What the hell does it mean? Life is the longest damn thing anyone ever does! Are they going to do something that's longer?"

"If it's got tits or tyres, you're gonna have trouble with it."

"We all have our disappointments in life, son, and I'm talking to mine right now."

"Life sucks, then you die."

"Remember the old gardening maxim: before you can come up smelling of roses you need to have been buried up to your neck in horse shit."

"The only way in which life resembles a bed of roses is that you encounter a lot of pricks along the way."

"What makes you think you're unpopular? I'm sure plenty of people have to organize their own surprise birthday party."

"So hardly anyone remembered your birthday? That doesn't mean you're unpopular. Listen, people lead busy lives – they have a lot of things to remember. They may not actually have forgotten your birthday – they may just have been preoccupied. They were probably thinking of you all the time. But in any case, you've always got your mother and me. Anyway when was your birthday? Oh, it's today. Right."

"Sure I'm surprised you can't get a job, son. I heard the world was crying out for someone who's lazy, has no qualifications but can spit gum into a waste-paper basket from ten feet."

"Don't you think you might stand a better chance of becoming a captain of industry if you got rid of some of that metal shit on your body – like the nose stud and the eyebrow rings? Donald Trump may have a crap haircut but I bet he doesn't have pierced fucking nipples."

"Your boss will always give you a hard time. That's what they're put on Earth for – that and to screw their secretary."

"Your job sucks?! My job sucked! Linda Lovelace's job sucked!"

"Nobody likes having to get up early for work on winter mornings, but we've all had to do it. Now I'm no expert political analyst but I'd hazard a guess that with all the problems in the world facing the new administration – Islamic terrorists, North Korea, the economic crisis – scrapping winter because you can't be bothered to get your fat ass out of bed in the morning probably comes pretty low down on their list of priorities."

"I'm sure they'll appreciate the supreme effort you're making by going to work in the snow. What do you think you'll get by way of reward – a pay increase, promotion, company car? It wouldn't surprise me if they make you CEO. Hell, it's half a dozen flakes of snow! It hasn't even settled on the ground. There's not enough to give frostbite to a fly, so I don't think we'll be seeing skiers and teams of huskies along the High Street just yet."

"You want to borrow some money, huh? You fucking little parasite. That's why this planet has things called jobs."

"You say you're afraid of being too successful too soon? Trust me, you have nothing to worry about."

"So you reckon you're bound to have a successful career because cream always rises to the top? That's true, it does – but then again, so does scum."

"Sorry but you just have to accept that the older you get, the tougher it is to lose weight, because by then your body and your fat have become really good friends."

"So you're having a bad hair day! Big deal! Every day of my life's been a bad hair day."

"Nobody's happy with what's on their head. People with straight hair want it to be curly, people with curly hair want it to be straight; people with blond hair want to be brunettes and people with dark hair want to be blondes;

people with ginger hair feel persecuted and bald people want everyone to be blind."

"You bought a car for five hundred bucks but it ain't running too good? Quelle fucking surprise! You're lucky it's running at all. What did you expect for five hundred bucks – leather interior, built-in mini bar and studio-quality sound system? It's probably only the Garfield on the side window that's holding the rustbucket together."

"Yeah, I agree with you; the guy in front is a lousy driver. The secret is to give him plenty of room to behave like a prick and not get so close to his rear end, like you are now, that you can almost smell what he had for lunch."

"So you reckon three speeding tickets in the past month are proof that you're being victimized? You don't think they could be proof that you drive too fast?"

"Don't get too cocky. If everything's coming your way, it usually means you're driving in the wrong lane."

"Have you ever heard of Sod's Law? It governs everything and dictates that anything that can go wrong will go wrong. For instance, it was Sod's Law that you were born when your mother and I desperately wanted a girl."

"The quickest way to make a red light turn green is to start looking for something in the glove compartment."

"The slowest drivers in the world are those people who are getting out of the parking space you're waiting to get into."

"As soon as you get a cup of coffee, your boss will send you on an errand that will last until the coffee is cold."

"If you tell your boss that you were late for work because of a flat tyre, it will be Sod's Law that the next morning you really will get a flat tyre."

"Your schooldays were the best days of your life. You remember when you were five and you pissed yourself in the school playground? Well, that was as good as it gets."

"Next time you wish you were young again, just think back to algebra homework."

"You had to wait over an hour to catch the bus to work this morning? That's terrible. What a waste of your valuable time. Think how many levels of *Assassin's Creed II* you could have played in that time."

"Accept it, you screwed up. Now let's move on. It's not the restaurant's fault that you booked for 7.30 but really meant 8.30. They're not mind-readers. It's a popular place, so of course they've let your table go. You can argue with them all you want but it won't get you anywhere. It's not like you're a major food critic with a bit of clout. You're just a guy who takes his old mum and dad out every Christmas to compensate for them having to put up with his shit the other fifty-one weeks of the year."

"As they said in *Forrest Gump,* life is like a box of chocolates – you never know what you're going to get. Just try not to get the nut cluster, sweetheart, because they always get stuck in your teeth."

"Life is not like a box of chocolates, life is like a shit sandwich. But the more bread you have, the less shit you have to eat."

"Life is like eating artichokes – you have to go through so much to get so little."

"Life is like a roll of toilet paper – the closer it gets to the end, the faster it goes."

"As Alan Bennett once said, life is like opening a tin of sardines – we're all of us looking for the key."

"I don't know why you're feeling so sorry for yourself. What about me? Last week I did one of those travel surveys where they have age bracket tick-boxes. The top age bracket was '60–75', but I had to put 'over 75' and it made me realize I am just one tick-box away from death."

"If you think there is good in everybody, you haven't met everybody."

"Stress, my arse! What have you got to be stressed about? If you did a proper man's job, like a fireman or a policeman or a surgeon, maybe I could understand it, but what stress is there involved with being a ladies' fucking hairdresser? What's the worst you can do to anyone? Give them an unsatisfactory blow dry?"

"Remember, if the world didn't suck, we'd all fall off."

"Builders never turn up on time – it's written in the code of the Federation of Master Builders. They operate on a different clock from the rest of the population. In fact, you're lucky they've shown up at all. Why do you think Rome wasn't built in a day? Because J.L. Gregory & Sons were on that job."

"We're all born naked, wet and hungry. And from then on, things just get worse."

"So you can't go to the game tomorrow night because your nasty old boss is making you work late? Sorry, but you're mistaking me for someone who gives a damn."

"Why are you so fucking miserable about hitting forty? It happens to us all. Do you think you're suddenly going to wake up tomorrow morning with a bald patch and a bad back? Don't even think about needing to 'slow down' as you put it. You've used up so little energy over the past thirty-nine years that you should have plenty in reserve to see you through a few more decades."

"You're feeling down because all you've got to show for forty years on Earth is a broken marriage? What about your police record? Don't forget that."

"If life was fair, Elvis would still be alive and all the impersonators would be dead."

"It's a fact that life's unfair. The best you can hope for is that it will occasionally be unfair in your favour."

"If life was fair, Scarlett Johansson would be begging me to take her out to a bar and a club and show her a good time. Instead, I've got to take your mother to bingo."

"If life was fair, men would get pregnant too."

"If life was fair, wasps would only sting bankers, lawyers, politicians and the bastard who wrote 'tosser' in the dirt on the side of my car."

"The secret of a happy life is to run out of cash and air at exactly the same time."

"The loan shark's interest rates are extortionate? No kidding! And now he's sending threatening letters because you can't keep up with the repayments? What did you expect to get from him – a Christmas card?"

"Your lottery numbers came up the one week you didn't buy a ticket? Gee, that's lousy luck. I guess there's a moral in there somewhere, and I think the moral is: you're a loser."

"Sure you can have a house party. But be warned: I'll wander around naked, telling all your friends embarrassing stories about your childhood."

"You're only young and stupid once. After that you're just stupid."

"There's always a lot to be thankful for if you just take the trouble to look for it. For example, I'm sitting here thinking how good it is that wrinkles don't hurt."

"Always try and look on the bright side of life, and if you can't find it, just get pissed."

"I always take life with a pinch of salt . . . plus a slice of lemon . . . and a shot of tequila."

# 2

# When I Was Your Age . . .

*Apart from receiving a new hip from Santa, there are few things old people relish more than the opportunity to stroll – slowly and three abreast so that they block the pavement – down memory lane. In the blink of a cataract they are transported back in time to a world of outside toilets, tin bathtubs, radio ventriloquists, nit nurses and bread and dripping, where everyone was so poor that the only hot meal they'd get was if a tramp was sick over them.*

"When I was your age, we didn't have fake dog shit. We only had real dog shit, and no one thought it was a damn bit funny."

"For Christmas, we'd get a pair of pants with a hole in the

pocket. That way, we'd have something to wear and something to play with."

"Listen, when I was a kid the nearest we got to a Jacuzzi was if one of us farted in the fucking bath."

"We were so poor when I was young that for Christmas dinner we used to go to the nearest KFC and lick other people's fingers."

"You're lucky even to have a toilet. When I was your age, we had to use a hole in a tree and take our chances with the local squirrels."

"I know it's bad that the hand drier in the toilet is broken, but in my day we didn't have such things. If I needed to dry my hands with hot air, I had to knee your father sharply in the balls."

"What are you wasting your money on aftershave for? In my day we used to stick on a bit of TCP."

"Is it true that on cable TV they have a channel devoted solely to the weather – twenty-four hours of weather? When I was a kid we had something like that, but we called it a window."

"You call these knickers? There's hardly enough material in them to cover a gnat's arse! You hang them on the line and they're smaller than the clothes peg! In my day, knickers were the size of small battleships and you wore them for twenty years before cutting them up to use as dusters."

"We didn't do all this keep-fit malarkey in my day. We got our exercise by carrying Uncle Albert back from the pub every night."

"You kids ain't mean. Heck, when I was growing up we didn't steal hub caps, we stole knee caps."

"Why do you kids have to go to the gym to exercise? In my day we kept fit by running from the cops."

"Safe sex? When I was your age, safe sex was when your grandma didn't know about it."

"I don't get the craze among youngsters for collecting these scratch and sniff stickers. Scratch and sniff used to be something you did to your butt."

"The problem is people these days are too comfortable. They don't know the meaning of suffering and hardship. If you ask me, everyone needs to go outside at least once in their life and take a good crap in the woods."

"When I was a kid, every house in the street had an outside toilet. I was thirteen before I knew what it was like to have a pee without icicles forming on the end of my dick."

"There's you fretting about what colour to paint the walls of your house! In my day, paint was for rich people. We had to decorate using the blood my brothers and I coughed up from breathing in dust all day long. And if we ran short, my father would slash his arm. So wherever we lived we had red walls. But we were happy."

"We were so poor that if shit were money, my dad would have been born without an asshole."

"What's all this bollocks about stress in the workplace? In my day you went to work even if you had an ear hanging off or were swathed from head to foot in bandages, and anyone who said he felt under pressure emotionally would likely be locked away in a secure unit for the rest of his life."

"I don't understand why women are always complaining about sexual harassment at work. In my day we complained if we didn't get any!"

"What's with all this health and safety crap? I don't know what the world's coming to. In my day, you could lose an arm at work and nobody batted an eyelid. In fact, you'd have to wait until the next tea break before they even called a doctor."

"Fuck health and safety. If these fuckwits had been around when I was a kid, we wouldn't even have been able to play snakes and fucking ladders in case we were somehow traumatised by a picture of a fucking cartoon snake on a piece of fucking card. 'Oh, Johnny's having terrible nightmares because if he ever goes anywhere near a ladder he thinks a giant anaconda's going to get him.' Send for social services."

"You call this music? You can't even understand the words! We had proper music in my day. Italian opera was my favourite."

"Back when I was a kid in the 1960s, we had real music – people like The Beatles, The Rolling Stones, The Beach Boys and . . . Cilla Black. Yeah, well not everything was great."

"All this screeching and shouting you get on songs these days, it's terrible. We had singers with beautiful clear voices, like the Singing Nun. Lovely voice she had. Pure and clean. Topped herself in a double suicide pact with her lesbian lover, you know."

"That's not dancing. That's an impression of someone having an epileptic fit. With moves like that, you wouldn't have lasted ten seconds on the floor of the old Mecca Ballroom in Southampton."

"You reckon I was strict? Well, when I was a boy, my father used to ground me – and then run electricity through me."

"The schools today are too soft. Our school was so tough it had its own coroner."

"There's so much violence on TV these days. Almost every programme seems to feature guns, and it sets kids such a bad example. Why can't they show a good Western instead?"

"Laura, I don't know why you're getting so worked up about not being able to find anything to wear. You've got a whole wardrobe full of clothes. When I was a girl, I had one dress – and that used to double up as a curtain at night."

"You call this beer? We gave stuff like this to babies."

"In my day, commitment to a relationship was emotional, financial and material. Nowadays commitment begins and ends with having your partner's name tattooed on your backside."

"How can you be bored? When I was your age I was never bored. We couldn't afford any toys, so we made our own entertainment. We'd play for hours beating each other black and blue with sticks and throwing stones at neighbours' windows, seeing how many we could smash. Ah, happy days!"

"Boredom? When I was your age I didn't know the meaning of the word 'boredom'. We couldn't afford a dictionary, you see."

"No, I never did weed. Well, just once. That shit will kill you. Just so that you know, I was drunk at the time."

"I never did coke. The only thing I ever want to put up my nose is my finger."

"Your grandma and I were so stick skinny, I'm amazed we didn't start a fire when we had sex."

"You reckon you can run fast? You don't know the meaning of fast. When I was your age I was so fast I could turn out the lights and get in bed before it went dark."

"We couldn't afford shoes, so we went barefoot. In the winter we had to wrap our feet with barbed wire for traction."

"We didn't have fancy shampoos. If anyone had dandruff, they were decapitated on the spot."

"In my day, we didn't have MTV or in-line skates, or any of that stuff. No, it was 45s and regular old metal-wheeled roller skates, and the 45s always skipped, so that to get them to play right you'd weigh the needle down with something like pennies, which we never had because our parents couldn't afford to give us an allowance, so we'd use our skate keys instead and end up forgetting they were taped to the record-player arm so that we couldn't adjust our skates, which didn't really matter because those crummy metal wheels would kill you if you hit a pebble anyway, and in those days roads had real pebbles in them, not like today . . ."

"No one had cars. If you wanted to get run over, you had to live on a tram route."

"We didn't have rocks. We had to go down to the creek and wash our clothes by beating them with our heads."

"Our house was so small that half of the TV was in one room and the other half was in another."

"When I was your age, everyone in the house had to share. I was only able to keep warm in bed at night if it wasn't the dog's turn for the blanket."

"We didn't have dogs or cats. The only pet I had was Silver Beauty, my beloved paperclip."

"We didn't have horses. We had to sew two ponies together."

"If I was five minutes late for work, the boss would brand me on both legs with a red-hot iron, stretch me on the rack for half an hour and then throw me in a vat of acid. And it never did me any harm."

"Kids today think the world revolves around them. In my day, the sun revolved around the world, and the world was perched on the back of a giant tortoise."

"When I was your age, we didn't have any Nintendo. We played real games like chew the bark off a tree. You played until your gums bled."

"When I was a kid we didn't have no fancy contraceptives like pullin' out."

"When I was your age, it cost more to run a car than it did to park it."

"We were so poor we had to use cobwebs for curtains."

"When I was a kid, I had to walk two miles to school every day through three feet of snow carrying two sacks of potatoes on my back."

"When I was a boy, I had to walk barefoot to school for four miles every day through five feet of snow carrying my school desk on my back and a bucketful of water in each hand."

"When I was young, I had to walk ten miles uphill to school every day through seven feet of snow carrying 1,200 pounds of firewood on my back and two bucketfuls of sand in each hand while rabid wolverines nipped at my elbows."

"Back when I was a boy, I had to walk fifteen miles to school every day through the snow – uphill both ways."

"Why don't you want to know how much a loaf of bread used to cost in my day? That's the trouble with you – you're just not interested in history."

"So there's no milk in the fridge?! Walk to the supermarket. It's all of two minutes away. In my day, if we ran out of milk we had to wait for your grandma to give birth again."

"We never had any of this virtual reality. If a one-eyed, green gargantuan monster was chasing you with an axe, you just had to hope you could outrun him."

"When I was your age, we couldn't afford to repair the large hole in the roof of our house. So whenever rain was forecast, we used to nail Grandma and Grandpa to the tiles and stretch them across the gap. They were always happy to help out."

"You kids have it so easy today. When I was your age there was no TV. If we wanted medical drama, we couldn't watch shows like *ER* – we had to perform our own open-heart surgery on Uncle Sidney in the living room."

"In my day, we didn't get that disembodied, slightly ticked-off voice saying 'Doors Closing'. We got on the train, the doors closed, and if your hand was sticking out it scraped along the tunnel all the damn way to the next station, by which time it was just a bloody stump. But the base fare was only a dollar."

"When I was your age, the house we lived in was so small that the front and back doors were on the same hinge."

"We didn't have hand-held calculators. We had to do addition on our fingers. To subtract, we had to have some fingers amputated."

"In my day, we didn't have water. We had to smash together our own hydrogen and oxygen atoms."

# 3

# Shut Your Face And
# Listen to Me

*Old people seem to think that living to the age of seventy automatically imbues them with enormous wisdom, which it is their duty to pass on to younger generations, not so much in the form of gentle suggestions, more as a modern version of the Ten Commandments. Well, giant tortoises live to the age of 150 but nobody has ever asked one for career advice, fashion tips or to propose a solution to the Middle East crisis. The truth is that most old people just like the sound of their own voice – that's if they're not too deaf to hear it.*

"There are two kinds of people in this world – the fuckers and the fuckees. Which would you rather be?"

"I'm not yelling at you. I'm helping you to hear."

"Always carry a litterbag in your car. It doesn't take up much space, and besides, when it gets full you can just toss it out the window."

"Never kick a turd on a hot day."

"Don't get in over your head. If you're gonna run with the big dogs, you gotta learn how to pee in the tall grass."

"Make sure anything you buy me is something you like, because you're getting it back when I die."

"Be careful – the toes you step on today may be connected to the ass you have to kiss tomorrow."

"Gossip is like a fart. Once it's out, you never know where it will spread or who it's gonna hit."

"Money's not like your pecker, son – it won't grow in your hands."

"You want my top tip for when you're feeling shit? Wear gloves."

"When you've got your head up your arse, all you see is shit."

"If you don't use your head, you might as well have feet at both ends."

"Some things simply aren't worth bothering with. You can tell the dog that it's highly embarrassing to sniff your Aunt Mabel like that till you're blue in the face, but he won't store it in his memory bank. He won't think, 'I'm showing myself up by doing that. In future I must behave with greater decorum.' Instead, the next time she comes to visit, you can guarantee his nose will be straight up her crotch as soon as she sits down."

"The only time the world beats a path to your door is when you're in the bathroom."

"Be totally ruthless in business and never cook bacon naked."

"Potatoes wrapped in tin foil and stored in a cupboard provide a welcome consolation if ever your house burns down."

"Think of how stupid the average person is, and then realize that half of them are stupider than that."

"Always look out for number one and be careful not to step in number two."

"If it floats, flies or fucks – rent it, don't buy it."

"If you're riding ahead of the herd, take a look back every now and then to make sure it's still there."

"Never put off dealing with something bad. A pile of shit will still be a pile of shit tomorrow and the day after – it ain't gonna suddenly change into a bouquet of flowers."

"If you're staying in a house with no toilet paper, it's not the end of the world. You can always slide down the banister."

"You can drink as much as you want, sweetheart. It's a fact that pretty girls do not throw up."

"If you want to get a good run for your money, eat prunes."

"Blood is thicker than water, and much more difficult to get out of the carpet."

"No one wins in a fight. If you hit him twenty times and he hits you once it still fucking hurts."

"If you ever get into a scrap, remember his bollocks are just as soft as yours."

"Remember, son, a crowded elevator always smells different to a midget."

"If the shoe fits, get another one just like it."

"A man never truly realizes how cold his hands are until he has to pee."

"If you're riding a bicycle down a hill, always remember to turn your head before you spit."

"If you think you're a person of some influence in this world, try ordering someone else's dog around."

"It's true that you can't take it with you, but you can hide it where no other bastard can find it."

"Be kind to your knees; you'll miss them when they're gone."

"The grass may look greener on the other side, but that could be because it's thicker and more difficult to mow."

"Don't drink and park. Accidents cause people."

"Early to bed and late to rise,
"And your girl goes out with other guys."

"God gave you two ears and one mouth. You should listen twice as much as you talk."

"Don't say blah-blah, when blah will do."

"A bird in the hand is safer than one overhead."

"A bird in the hand makes it darned near impossible to blow your nose."

"You watch how you go there, boy, because in my

experience trouble always starts out looking like fun."

"The only substitute for good manners is fast reflexes."

"Always wear clean underwear in case you get in an accident."

"If you're up to your neck in shit, there's not much point in slinging it."

"Everyone seems normal – until you get to know them."

"Light travels faster than sound, which is why some people appear bright until you hear them speak."

"Drink till she looks cute, but stop before the wedding."

"Listen to Grandma: eat up all your broccoli – it will make your hair grow. If you want to know what happens to people who don't eat their broccoli, just take a look at Grandpa."

"Never look at a woman while she's eating a banana."

"Never hit a man with glasses. Hit him with something bigger and heavier."

"When it comes to cars, choose big. Horsepower is like a condom: it's better to have it and not need it than to need it and not have it."

"Drive carefully. It's not only cars that can be recalled by their maker."

"When you're drunk or if you've just woken up in the middle of the night and you're not sure where you are but you need a piss, sit on the bog like a woman. You'll save yourself a lot of trouble."

"Always drink upstream from the herd."

"You think it's just coincidence that your boss happened to walk in while you had your feet on the desk reading *Playboy*? Don't you believe it; these things happen for a reason. Coincidence is God's way of remaining anonymous."

"Always make a point of befriending a recovering alcoholic. That way you'll never be short of a ride home."

"When you're arguing with an idiot, try to make sure he isn't doing the same thing."

"If it's a choice between saving your face and saving your arse, always save your arse. Otherwise how will you shit?"

"Cheer yourself up at the next funeral you go to by hiding a twenty-pound note in your black suit today."

"People who live in glass houses might as well answer the door."

"Don't kick a man when he's down, unless you're absolutely certain he won't get up."

"I've always said that the best way to stop your children being spoilt is to keep them in the fridge."

"Be wary of strong drink. It can make you shoot at tax collectors – and miss."

"Once society collapses, the only three commodities will be guns, booze and women. And he who has the guns and booze will get the women."

"If you want to forget all your troubles, buy a pair of tight shoes."

"It doesn't pay to be too modest in life. A peacock who sits on his tail is just another turkey."

"If you eat a cup full of earwax first thing every morning, nothing worse will happen to you for the rest of the day."

"Knowledge is knowing a tomato is a fruit; wisdom is not putting it in a fruit salad."

"If duct tape don't fix it, you ain't using enough duct tape."

"Always push yourself to go that extra mile. You'll be surprised what you can achieve. It's like wiping your ass. You think it's clean but if you carry on wiping, you can always find a little more."

"Excuses are like backsides. Everybody's got one and they all stink."

"People will believe anything if you whisper it."

"Don't focus on the one guy who hates you; think about all the ones who are indifferent towards you."

"I'm sure it's not true that everyone hates you. How can they? They haven't all met you yet."

"Don't antagonise your boss, just keep your head down. The more you stir a turd the worse it stinks."

"Why does everyone get so worked up about getting old? Age doesn't matter – unless you're a fine wine or a cheese."

"I'm seventy-three, but I prefer to think of myself as 23 Celsius."

"You'll be old one day – and maybe before you know it because old age is like underwear; it creeps up on you."

"You know how exciting it is shopping for a new car? Well, when you get to my age you shop like that for health insurance."

"You can't drink as much when you get to my age. To me, happy hour is a nap."

"It's not all bad being old. For a start, there's nothing left to learn the hard way."

"Another good thing about living into your nineties is that you can be crap at golf but still shoot your age."

"Golf and fishing are the two finest sports a man can enjoy. You can do both until you die, and both allow you to open your first beer at seven o'clock in the morning."

"Never hunt anything smarter than you. Perhaps in your case you should try hunting worms."

"If you ever find yourself being kidnapped, shit your pants. The kidnappers won't take you then."

"No matter how tempting it may look, never try to sharpen a pencil up a cat's arse."

"Never throw a brick or an angry cat straight up in the air."

"No matter how cold it is, never invite the cat to sleep under the sheets in your bed – especially if you are naked."

"You could be right, sweetheart; the cat may well be smiling at you. On the other hand, it's the same expression he has when he's about to launch a savage, unprovoked attack on your ankle."

"Always be nice to your sister – you might need an alibi some day."

"He who laughs last at the boss's jokes probably isn't far from retirement."

"No matter how tempting it is to be at one with nature, stay on the outside of all fences at the zoo."

"Always keep your words soft and sweet, just in case you have to eat them."

"On the keyboard of life, always keep one finger on the Escape key."

"The best things in life aren't always free. For instance, if you want to chew gum, buy some. Don't use the gum from underneath seats at schools and movie theatres."

"If you're looking to raise money through medical science, sell at most just one of your kidneys."

"A friend is someone you can call to help you move. A best

friend is someone you can call to help you move a body."

"If you accidentally shit your pants, blame the dog. It works for me."

"You can tell a lot about a person from two things – the inside of their refrigerator and the inside of their car."

"Everything you need to know in life you can learn from *Star Trek* and the Bible – in that order."

"If you can keep your head while others around you are losing theirs, you may want to land your helicopter someplace else."

"When people say 'Don't try this at home,' what they really mean is 'Don't try this at all. Anywhere'."

"You can lose money chasing women, but you'll never lose women chasing money."

"Worrying is like a rocking chair. It gives you something to do, but it doesn't get you anywhere."

"Candy is dandy but liquor is quicker."

"Always vote first thing in the morning, because if in the course of the day you step off the kerb and get run over by a three-ton truck, your vote still counts."

"Listen, honey, women will never be equal to men until they can walk down the street with a bald head and a beer gut, and still think they're sexy."

"Don't put all your eggs in one basket. If a bloody chicken can work that out, so can you."

"We can't all be fucking heroes. Someone has to stand on the pavement and clap as they pass by."

"Anything's possible – except maybe for skiing through a revolving door."

"One day you'll learn that if you take care of things before they become a problem, they won't become a problem in the first place. Although if we had followed that reasoning, you wouldn't be here anyway."

"Don't do drugs. They'll wreck your body – and I might need one of your organs some day."

"Never give yourself a haircut after three margaritas."

"No one is listening until you fart."

"It's always darkest before dawn. So if you're going to steal your neighbour's milk, that's the time to do it."

"Remember: it takes forty-two muscles to frown but only four to pull the trigger of a decent sniper rifle."

"As you journey through life, take a moment every now and then to think about others – because there's every chance they could be plotting something."

"Three is the magic number in life. You'll die in three minutes without oxygen, three days without water, three weeks without food, and three months without sex."

# 4

# You Gotta Respect Me – I'm a Senile Citizen

*A senior citizen with a grievance is never likely to be mistaken for a ray of sunshine – as any stranger who has innocently sat in Old Harry's favourite chair at the pub will testify. An irate pensioner might scar someone for life verbally – or physically if a walking cane is handy – but will expect to be excused such behaviour because he or she is considered a "character", presumably in the same way that Vlad the Impaler considered himself to be a character. Any further attempt at remonstration will be met by the playing of the "doolally" card, whereby said old person cites a bad memory, failing eyesight and general confusion as the reasons for having nailed your hand to the bar.*

"My memory's starting to go. Just about the only thing I still retain is water."

"Today I did that thing where you walk into a room and totally forget what you went in for. It was only when the shit started trickling down my leg that I remembered."

"I'll never forget when I lost *my* virginity. It was just after the war. His name was David. Or was it Derek?"

"My memory's not what it was. I keep forgetting things. It's like I've got Eisenhower's."

"Sorry, what were you talking about just now? Oh yes, Alzheimer's."

"I'm suffering from Mallzheimer's. I go to the shopping mall and forget where I parked my car."

"The face is familiar but I can't remember my name."

"Your grandfather keeps forgetting where he's left his teeth. We call them his dementia dentures."

"What happened in 1953? Apart from the Coronation. Something happened to me. Something to do with a hospital I think . . . You say you were born in 1953? Oh yes, that must be it: I had you. See, I told you something happened to me that year."

"So that's how the microwave works? You learn something every day. The trouble is you forget it every night."

"I'll tell you why I love watching repeats of shows like *Midsomer Murders*, *Miss Marple* and *Murder She Wrote* – because even half an hour after the end credits I can never remember whodunit."

"The good thing about going senile is everything's funny all over again."

"Who was that actress that used to be on TV in the

seventies? Pert little thing. In that comedy series. You know the one. There were four of them – two men and two women. What was her name? She went on to appear on that dancing show with Bruce Forsyth. I can picture her face. It'll come to me. I remember . . . Facility Kendal."

"I saw thingy last week, oh whatshername, I don't know, I can never remember anything these days – it's this damn anorexia."

"What was the name of that man who used to give you driving lessons? Keith somebody. Keith . . . Oh, it's on the tip of my tongue. Keith . . . Keith . . . John Miller, that's it."

"I bumped into whatshername this morning at the bus station. Used to live along the road, she was friends with the barmaid at the pub. Oh, what's her name? You know who I mean – cropped hair, crooked teeth, big arse."

"I'm sorry, I've completely forgotten your name. No, wait, it's Jim, isn't it? No? Jack? No? John? Oh, you say it's Jeremy? Yes, of course it is. It's come back to me now. I knew we should have christened you something that was easier to remember."

"I always know my secrets are safe with your grandpa because he can't remember them either."

"How can I be over the hill? I don't remember being on top of it."

"Have you seen the TV remote anywhere? I swear I saw it only five minutes ago . . . Oh, it's okay, I found it . . . Can you remember where I said I'd found it?"

"I wanna tell you a joke, but it's kind of racist, so I'll leave the racist part out. Okay? A black man, a white man and a Chinese man walk into a bar . . .

"I'll tell you why they put cartoons on TV – it's so that the actors can have a break."

"In my day we used to do the jitterbuggery until the early hours of the morning. Your grandfather used to love doing the jitterbuggery."

"I'm not sure I can walk all the way around the lake at my age. So if I get halfway round and feel too tired, I'll just come back."

"You gotta be more decisive, boy. It's time to grab the bull by the tail and look him in the eye."

"George, did you read in the paper that France has got a new nuclear detergent?"

"Mildred's having problems with her vision. I think the doctor said she's got a detached rectum."

"Don't worry, dear. We'll burn that bridge when we get to it."

"Where's my other earring? Oh, I don't know. It's probably somewhere in the mashed potato."

"Wow! Have you seen that young man over there? He's absolutely drop-down gorgeous."

"I'm so busy, I don't know whether I'm coming or not."

"No wonder Joseph and Mary couldn't find any room at the inn. Everywhere was busy. They should have known it's always busy at Christmas."

"Don't look at me in that tone of voice."

"Why didn't you tell me you were taking me to a smart hotel? If I'd known we were going somewhere nice, I would have put on a bra."

"So, David, how are you coping with your necrophilia these

days? Okay, okay, so it's called narcolepsy. Anyone can make a mistake."

"A sexagenarian? At his age? I think that's disgusting."

"It could be that his past has finally caught up with him. It looks like the cows have come home to roost."

"You say the bailiffs are at the door? That's the last straw! George, how many times have I told you to let me know beforehand when you've invited friends round for lunch! I haven't got anything in at all. The least you can do is invite Mr and Mrs Bailiff in while I put the kettle on."

"Why should I tread carefully around him just because he's autistic? I can draw, too, you know!"

"Yes, Stonehenge is truly awesome, George, but there's one thing I just don't understand. Why did they build it so close to the main road?"

"You're from America? How lovely. Do you know a man called Richard in Los Angeles? He's my cousin."

"Your grandpa and me are going to Australia next month. We're flying with Quaintass."

"Do you know there are places in space that are even farther away than Australia?"

"I'd like an aisle seat on the plane if possible – so that my hair won't get messed up by being near the window."

"Nine hours that plane journey took. I can't tell you how good it is to be back on terra cotta."

"My granddaughter's going to Japan next month. I think she wants to see the Great Wall of China."

"It's not the heat that I can't bear in Spain – it's the humility."

"Why do you want to go to Lapland? That's where they do all that lap dancing, isn't it?"

"Well, I'm a little more enlightened than you, Mildred, so I'd really like to go to Lapland. Tell me, young man, is Lapland open every day and are the queues long?"

"Why do so many people object to lap dancing? I remember when Sammy Davis Jr and Roy Castle used to do it on TV. It was just a lot of clicking heels. Perfectly harmless."

"I heard some lad at the drugstore say our Debbie's a carpet muncher. That'll be one of those crazy diets the kids go on these days."

"Food doesn't grow on trees, you know!"

"Excuse me, dear. Can you tell me what time the four o'clock ferry leaves?"

"So I sent you a Deepest Sympathy card for your birthday? What's the problem? I liked the flower on the front."

"I chose this birthday card especially for you, Jason, because there's a picture of a keyboard on the front, and I know how much you love your music . . . Have I read the words inside? No, I haven't. Why? Let's have a look. It says: 'Happy birthday. Tonight we could make beautiful music together, just you and me . . . and your organ.' "

"Did you see that item on the news where the prisoners climbed on to the roof of the jail, ripped off all the lead and started throwing it at the warders below? If you ask me they want locking up!"

"I'm not getting involved. The argument's between you and your sister. I don't want to be the one to upset the apple tart."

"I'll tell you one of the key things that I've learned from life, boy: when you come to a fork in the road, take it."

"That woman's so dumb, she doesn't have two brains to rub together."

"Hey, buddy, where do you keep the Fred Zeppelin albums in this place?"

"Let me show you what I bought the other day. It's one of those new George Formby grills."

"Jean next door drives me crazy. I know she's eighty-four, but that's only a few years older than me. But she's grumpy, she's rude and she's always repeating herself. And she's grumpy and rude."

"You won't catch me going to church – not with the smell of all that incest."

"Yes, I know my hair's getting too long. Don't worry, I've booked in tomorrow at that new place in the High Street for a cut and blow job. Do you think I'll have to pay extra for the blow job?"

"This drawer keeps sticking. Have we got any of that UB40?"

"George, do you know whether they have New Year's Day in Canada?"

"Ah, so you must be Jonathan, my granddaughter's boyfriend. I don't believe you've had the pleasure of me yet."

"My granddaughter's crazy. She's fruitier than a nutcake."

"I don't understand her moods. One minute she's calm, the next she's all over the place. Her behaviour's very erotic."

"Help me out here, I'm not used to cooking. It says here to separate the eggs. How far apart do they have to be?"

"I can tell exactly what you're thinking. Just call me septic."

"Your car has got bigger since the last time I saw it . . . Oh, I see. It's a new car."

"Isn't it lovely seeing Paul and Emily together? Those two get on like a horse on fire."

"You didn't tell me Josh's girlfriend was ornamental . . . You know, ornamental . . . By the look of her she comes from China or Japan or one of those countries."

"He'll be hard pushed to get out of this mess. If you ask me, he's up a tree without a paddle."

"I do make mistakes, you know. I'm not inflammable."

"Have you seen those silly fools on the telly? Throwing themselves off bridges! You won't catch me doing any of that budgie jumping!"

"It's essential that we all stick together. That's why family bondage is so important."

"No, I'm fine now. It was just a shooting pain in my chest – probably an attack of vagina."

"It's two o'clock, time for my two-hour afternoon nap. So wake me when it's five o'clock."

"I may be getting on a bit, but I can still party like it's 1899."

"Careful when you use the toilet because I've poured in some of that new cleaner that gets rid of 99 per cent of all living orgasms around the house."

"That woman's wearing a wig . . . Yes, of course I'm sure. Mind you, it's a very good one. You'd never guess!"

"I've never been so disgusted in my life. I read in the TV

listings magazine that there was a new drama series – something about girls and love – so I thought it might be nice and heartwarming but in the very first scene there were two women touching each other with those diddalos."

"I'm not ready for the knacker's yard just yet, you know. I still know what's what. I'm still compost mentis."

"Excuse me, young man, I've locked my keys in my car and my two grandchildren are inside . . . Do I have a spare set? Yes, I have two more grandchildren who live in Australia."

"Your grandma has gone for a lie down because we've just come back from the doctor who has told her she's got very close veins."

"Don't expect sympathy from me. You buttered your bread. Now you'll have to sleep in it."

"I was driving home from the supermarket yesterday when

I was nearly run off the road by a trucker. Damn HIV drivers!"

"Hey, George, look at the moon over the Mississippi. That looks like the same moon we saw in England."

"Just wait till you see the picture on our TV. It's better than ever – it's one of those new ones with VD."

"Child abuse? What are you talking about – child abuse? You wouldn't know child abuse if it hit you!"

"Let me get this straight: you say you're going away for a romantic weekend with your workmate? Well, I always knew you were keen on DIY but I had no idea the feelings were that intense."

"You won't catch me eating any of that foreign muck. I'll just have a pizza, love."

"Did you see that car smash on TV last night? The driver got ejaculated right out of the window."


"We're on Route 25, officer? I thought that was the speed limit sign. I wondered why everyone was honking at me."


"I am worried about the effects of global warming, George. Does it mean that in twenty years there will be no ice for my gin and tonic?"


"I don't see what he's done wrong, dear. All he did was call the referee a wanker, whatever that means."


"If your granddad was alive today, he'd turn in his grave."


"Listen, sweetheart, you shouldn't get into water until you've learned to swim."


"George, do you know that feeling when you get popcorn stuck between your boobs?"

"Parents are so unimaginative with names. These days every Tom, Dick and Harry is called Jack."

"If you break both your legs, don't come running to me."

"What's so crazy about asking for two Seeing Eye Dogs? I wanted one for reading."

"Of course you can't see her, George – she's blind!"

"You say you're having a sweep to induce the baby? Well, that's a new one on me. I don't see how having a wager with the midwife about the baby's length and weight is gonna make things happen any quicker."

"Dear Sir, I wish to inform the council that my bush is really overgrown round the front and my back passage has fungus growing in it."

"I want some repairs done to my cooker as it has backfired and burnt my knob off."

"I wish to report that tiles are missing from the outside toilet roof. I think it was bad wind the other night that blew them off."

"It's the dogs' mess that I find hard to swallow."

"And their eighteen-year-old son is continually banging his balls against my fence."

"This is to let you know that our lavatory seat is broken and we can't get BBC2."

"I am writing on behalf of my sink, which is coming away from the wall."

"I am stunned that you are refusing to pay me out for this accident simply because I wasn't wearing my glasses. I swear that the accident was in no way my fault. I simply didn't see the cyclist when I ran him over."

"My car slowed down but the traffic was much more stationary than I thought it was."

"I collided with a tree that was stationary."

"I collided into a lamp-post that was obscured by a human being."

"The accident was caused by me waving to the man I hit last week."

"I left for work this morning at 7 a.m. as usual when I collided straight into a bus. The bus was five minutes early."

"The accident happened because I had one eye on the truck in front, one eye on the pedestrian, and the other on the car behind."

"So I dropped my glasses in my lap?! It doesn't mean I'm ready for the Sunnyview Retirement Home just yet. Maybe I just wanted to see what was going on in my vagina."

"I'm so confused I don't know whether to scratch my watch or wind my butt."

"Bless him, he's as confused as a baby in a topless bar."

"The nice thing about being senile is you can hide your own Easter eggs."

"So I forgot to indicate? Big deal! Listen, we've lived in the same road for over forty years, so I think people know where I'm going by now."

"At my age, 'getting lucky' means finding my car in the car park."

"You'll have to excuse your granddad. He always likes to

stop the microwave at one second because it makes him think he's back in the army defusing a bomb."

"I'll tell you the best thing about being old: I'm allowed to shit my pants."

"You wanna know why we've lived in the same house for forty-eight years? Because it's the one place where I can piss off the front porch without anyone seeing."

"I don't care if you do threaten to put me in a home. I'm telling you for the last time, I haven't got Mr Bun the Baker!"

## 5

# I Wouldn't Even Waste a Fart on Some Folks

*Let's be honest, some people are a waste of skin, but while the politically correct younger generation might fight shy of expressing their views too vehemently, old folks rarely feel under such constraints. They deliver put-downs with both barrels in a manner that makes Dorothy Parker sound like one of the Waltons. And forget the stuff about mellowing with age and letting bygones be bygones. Many old people still bear grudges from childhood, vilifying someone for life just because he once took their pencil sharpener.*

"I've not seen such a guilty face since I finished my jigsaw of O. J. Simpson."

"Why do people point at their wrist while asking for the time? I know where my watch is, buddy. Where the hell is yours? Do I point at my crotch when I ask where the bathroom is?"

"How come people are willing to get off their ass to search the entire room for the TV remote because they refuse to walk to the TV and change the channel manually?"

"Why don't you start using your head for something other than a hat rack?"

"She's the town gossip. She's like a woman with a paper asshole. Can't keep a damn thing in – it's just all gotta come right out."

"That woman just can't stop talking. She never shuts up. You ask her what the time is, and she'll tell you how to build a clock!"

"That guy talks such a load of shit – and he does it all day long. I bet if you taped his mouth shut, he'd fart himself to death."

"Oh, so he's a nice person once you get to know him? What you mean is, 'He's a total dickhead but you'll get used to it'."

"He calls himself a manager – he couldn't manage a half-decent shit."

"He's as useless as tits on a bull."

"That guy's about as useful as a pogo stick in quicksand."

"He's a self-made man, which shows what happens when you don't follow the directions."

"You know what I think his problem is? He got picked before he was ripe."

"He ain't worth a bucket of warm spit."

"He thinks he's better than everyone else around here. He thinks his craps don't stink, but his farts'll give 'em away."

"He's full of more shit than a constipated elephant."

"I refuse to play golf with that guy. If I want to play with a prick, I'll play with my own."

"If that guy was a liquid, he'd be dripping off a toilet brush."

"That boy should be a poster child for birth control."

"He's as flash as a rat with a gold tooth."

"If I had wanted to hear from an asshole, I would have farted."

"If brains were lard, he wouldn't have enough to grease a frying pan."

"He wouldn't have the sense to pour piss out of a boot with directions on the bottom."

"When I look at your cousin Joe, I think to myself, 'Some village is missin' their idiot'."

"That guy is so fucking ignorant, he doesn't know baby shit from butterscotch."

"I know you quite like the guy, but I'm afraid I couldn't warm to him even if I was cremated next to him."

"He's so stupid he couldn't find his ass with a flashlight and a road map."

"That guy is so mean, he's tighter than a camel's ass in a sandstorm."

"Unpopular? I'll say he's unpopular. If his circle of friends was any smaller, it would be a dot!"

"I need that guy as a boss about as much as a tomcat needs a marriage licence."

"That guy is too lazy to scratch his own backside."

"He's a waste of time, space, air, flesh, and the rectum he was born from."

"Trust me, there are plenty of adults who can't count to ten. I should know because I'm always stuck behind them in the supermarket express queue."

"We had four children – five if you count my ex-husband."

"I know your father's a total jerk, but I felt it was my duty to dilute the stupid gene."

"What was it like being married to your mother? Well, we shared a sense of humour, but then again we had to because she didn't have one."

"Don't you hate it when people say, while watching a movie, 'Did you see that?' 'No, dicknose, I paid nine dollars to come to the theatre and stare at the frigging ceiling up there. What did you come here for?'"

"Why do people say 'you're joking' when you tell them something serious? 'I've got cancer.' 'You're joking!' 'My mother died last night.' 'You're joking!' Sure, I always joke about stuff like that. Dead parents are a constant source of comic material. Oh, my aching sides!"

"Do me a favour. Put your lips over your head, and swallow."

# 6

# Always Date Ugly Chicks – They're Grateful

*Parents and grandparents can never be accused of sitting on the fence when it comes to dishing out relationship advice. As a general rule of thumb, men don't want their daughters going near any boy, but want their sons to shag everything in sight, except other boys. Women don't really mind if their sons are gay so long as their partner has good taste in soft furnishings, but demand that their daughters marry the first boy they meet who has decent prospects. If we're talking Jewish mothers or grandmothers, this means nothing less than a senior surgeon, the head of a law firm, or maybe, as a last resort, President of the United States.*

"Women are like shoes. You can try on all the shoes you

want, but just you remember – if you crap in 'em, you're gonna be buyin' 'em."

"You need to start dating sluttier-looking girls. That way when you bring them home I can start looking at them."

"I don't want to walk in again and find you and your girl making out on the couch – at least not without my video camera."

"Date dumb but marry smart – you'll have more fun that way."

"Don't marry for money – you can borrow it cheaper."

"Why don't you ask out that girl who works at Marks & Spencer? That way, if you don't like her, you can always exchange her."

"You think she's pretty? You should have gone to Specsavers."

"Yeah, I guess she's okay if you like your chicks to be homely, domestic and boring. She'll have your dinner waiting on the table when you get home from work but I wouldn't count on too much excitement in the bedroom department. Your mother will love her."

"Girlfriend? What girlfriend? The only girlfriend you've ever had was that blow-up doll you bought online. I'm talking about a real girl – one with a vulva not a valve."

"So you're off on a date with a girl? I didn't even know you had a girlfriend, and before you say anything relatives don't count."

"Sure you're going on a hot date – just like I'm really going into town tonight to make out with Jennifer Aniston instead of staying at home with a mug of cocoa and watching reruns of *Cagney and Lacey*."

"I'll tell you something, son, a girlfriend is like a credit card. If you have one, it's a whole lot easier to get a new one."

"Try dating homeless women. It's easier to talk them into staying over."

"Yes, I know I said girls always like flowers – but not when they're still attached to the rest of the wreath."

"You're getting engaged? About time too! No guy in his forties should still be single . . . Okay, sorry, my mistake. No guy in his thirties should still be single."

"I figure as long as you're not fucking fat chicks or shooting drugs up your nose, you could be doing a lot worse for yourself."

"You want my advice for the dance? Ignore the pretty girls and go ugly early to avoid disappointment."

"Son, let me pass on the wisdom of my experience: always be nice to women – even the ugly ones, because they have cute friends and they all talk to each other."

"Beauty is only skin deep; ugly goes right to the bone."

"It's an accepted truism that the uglier the girl, the closer she lives."

"Remember, she might not be a real looker but beauty is only a light-switch away."

"You've got to treat your girlfriend with respect. Call me old fashioned, but I'm not sure that posting pictures of her new breast implants on the Internet necessarily does that."

"If you get a reputation for being able to eat pussy like a champ, you'll never go short of a date on a Saturday night."

"If you're not careful, by the time you're able to read a

girl like a book, your library card will have expired."

"Fill your boots while you can. When you're older, it'll be harder to get a bit of skirt."

"Women are like cowpats. The older they are, the easier they are to pick up."

"Sow your wild oats on Saturday night – then on Sunday pray for crop failure."

"If you fish in another man's well, you run the risk of catching crabs."

"You may get off on a cheap hooker, but you can't get off on a cheap lawyer."

"You know I'll support you whatever choices you make in life, son. Unless you marry the town slapper, in which case I'll disown you."

"She may be pretty, but in no circumstances should you ever let your little head take control from your big one."

"Never marry a woman with large hands. They make your dick look small."

"Here's some advice for you: if you ever wake up one morning, look across at the girl in your bed and wish you had an axe in your hand, it's probably best to get out of the relationship."

"Money can't buy you love, but it sure gets you a great bargaining position."

"If you want your wife to pay undivided attention to every word you say, start talking in your sleep."

"Your new girlfriend is thirty-eight, drop-dead gorgeous and has never been married? I hate to say it, son, but she sounds too good to be true. Next time you go round to her place, look out for blood stains on the carpet or a newly laid area of patio . . . just to be sure."

"On your first date with a girl you really like, the only thing you can count on is that at some point in the evening you will get a bad attack of gas. You sit at home all day, and you don't fart once. You go on a date and you've got twenty in the bank straight away."

"It's a shame you can't date girls on Amazon, because then they'd recommend who your next girlfriend should be, too."

"I never went for one-night stands. I think you should get to know someone and even be in love with them before you use them and degrade them."

"It's good to see you making an effort with this girl, Michael. Look after her and treat her with respect, even if she is trailer trash."

"For your first proper date together, you want to take her somewhere she'll feel at home. How about dog racing?"

"Son, you know what they say about faint heart never winning fair lady? Well, I expect that applies to Candy-Jo, too."

"If you really fancy the girl, go ahead, take the plunge, ask her for a date. Don't let your lack of education, style or good looks stand in the way."

"What's the worst she can do? The worst she can do is say 'no'. Okay, so I guess she could add that she wouldn't touch you with a barge pole if you were the last guy on Earth and that your breath stinks like a dead cat, but she'll probably settle for just saying 'no'."

"So you think this girl's too good for you? She'll probably come to the same conclusion soon enough anyway, but in the meantime don't make up her mind for her by behaving like a dork."

"Girls are like toilet cubicles. They're either taken or full of shit."

"Women are like jazz music – 3/4 jazz time and 1/4 rag time."

"Don't be blinded by big tits. You wouldn't buy a car just because it's got a big bonnet."

"No matter how good she looks, somebody is tired of putting up with her shit."

"Okay, so what other qualities does this girl have apart from banging like the toilet door on a trawler?"

"Remember, the first time you have sex, keep the receipt."

"When getting naked with a girl, always take your socks off as early as possible. Naked and erect while wearing only socks is not a sexy look."

"Never do anything in bed that you can't pronounce."

"When the weather is hot and sticky is not the time to dip
    your dicky;
"But when the frost is on the pumpkin, that's the time for
    dicky dunkin'."

"Flies carry disease. Keep yours closed, son."

"Make sure you remember to use protection. Put it on
before you put it in."

"Threesomes are fine in theory, but do you really want
to wake up the next morning with *two* disappointed
women?"

"Sex is not the answer. Sex is the question. 'Yes' is the
answer."

"If sex is a pain in the ass, you're doing it wrong."

"My father used to say to me: having sex is like playing

bridge. If you don't have a good partner, you'd better have a good hand."

"You'd better be using protection. Accidents happen. How do you think you got here?"

"Love is blind, but the neighbours aren't."

"Love may not be blind, but in your case, it's definitely in need of an eye test."

"All relationships go through rocky patches, boy. Hell, I've been in the doghouse so many times that when I meet another man I don't know whether to shake his hand or sniff his tail!"

"Here's a tip for you: never argue with a woman who is packing your parachute."

"There are two theories about arguing with women.

And I'm telling you now that neither theory works."

"When you're not in a relationship, try shaving one leg. That way, when you sleep it will feel like you're with a woman."

"Sorry your girlfriend dumped you . . . Oh, okay, it was a mutual decision to go your separate ways . . . but one that she suggested first. Sounds like a dumping to me."

"If it's of any consolation, I knew you weren't right for each other – and that was before I saw her snogging that young mechanic at the bus stop. Oh, sorry, you didn't know about that . . . Pretend I didn't say anything."

"She said you were more like a brother to her? Yeah, that's a line they often use to let you down gently. Not much consolation is it, unless she's really into incest?"

"Maybe deep down she really does love you. After all, I'm only an old fogey. What do I know? It's just that my experience of life has told me that girls tend to demonstrate their affection for their boyfriends with an expensive shirt or a watch rather than a restraining order."

"Never chase after a bus or a girl – another one'll come along soon enough."

"There's plenty more fish in the sea. Just don't let your rod go rusty."

"There's plenty more fish in the sea, which is quite apt seeing as how your ex had a face like a haddock. No offence."

"Does it really matter who dumped who, sweetheart? The end result is the same: you're another year nearer perpetual spinsterhood."

"Well, that's his loss, honey. Where else will he find another girl around here that goes like a rattlesnake?"

"I can't believe your boyfriend has ditched you, especially as your father has been secretly paying him £250 a month for the past year just to stay with you. I guess some people have no scruples."

"Sex is like snow, sweetheart. You never know how many inches you are going to get or how long it is going to last."

"Don't listen to those old fuddy-duddies who never let their partner see their body. There is absolutely nothing wrong with making love with the light on – just make sure the car door is closed."

"Darling, if you dress right, you should never have to pay for a night out at a bar. In fact, show a bit more tit and you may even make money."

"You never know when you're going to meet the special boy that you want to spend the rest of your life with. Love has a habit of creeping up your back and knocking your hat off."

"Never chase after a man – unless he's stolen your purse."

"This is so lovely to have our favourite granddaughter round for lunch. So tell me dear, are you still a virgin? Have you had your cherry popped? Would you like another slice of beef, George?"

"Don't be shy in bed, and always try to give the man what he wants. Don't forget, it's only kinky the first time you do it."

"Don't deny him sex just because it's the time of the month. My mother always told me: 'If the front porch is being painted, go in through the back'."

"The wife who puts her husband in the dog house will soon find him in the cat house."

"Sweetheart, I said you should play harder to get, not impossible. You know, there is a middle ground somewhere between Pamela Anderson and Mother Teresa."

"When I said you should play harder to get, I meant you shouldn't sit with your legs ninety degrees apart. In my day, sixty was always sufficient to give a boy a glimpse of the goods."

"I always remember what my own grandmother told me: if you get them by the balls, their hearts and minds will follow."

"You're young and beautiful. You should be having the time of your life. It's all very well staying in and studying but at your age you should be having an orgasm a day."

"You mean he actually asked you out for a second date? Wow! We'll have to stop calling you the One-Date Wonder behind your back."

"I was beginning to worry that you'd been left on the shelf so long you'd soon be covered in cobwebs."

"Don't be too choosy about boys, darling. Remember, men

are like parking spots – the good ones are already taken and the ones that are left are handicapped."

"Don't be shy about putting what you have to offer on display. A man will only enter a store if he likes what he sees in the window."

"I just don't think you should get serious with that boy – you'll have ugly children."

"Don't sleep around. A man will never buy the cow if he gets the milk for free."

"Stay a virgin as long as you can because take it from me, sex is like a can of Pringles. Once you pop, you just can't stop."

"Don't have sex before you get married because once you are married, he'll expect you to do it all the time."

"If you ever have sex with anybody rich and famous, make sure he impregnates you. Do you hear me?"

"Men are like cars – make sure you test drive them before you buy them."

"The best way to get over a guy is get under a new one."

"You better pay close attention to birth control, Jenny, because if the women in our family even so much as get a sniff of sperm, bang – they're pregnant!"

"A husband's attitude to sex with his wife is a bit like that of a dog with a bone; he might not touch it but he won't let other dogs come near it."

"Men have two emotions: hungry and horny. If you see him without an erection, make him a sandwich."

"Listen to your grandma: the best thing you can treat

yourself to is a good vibrator, because you'll find in married life that there are times when your husband just won't be able to do the business."

"I bought your mother a vibrator for her birthday once. She's done nothing but moan ever since."

"It's always the quiet ones that have half a dozen corpses in the basement."

"Who's being embarrassing? All I said was I don't want her giving her new boyfriend blow jobs – not after all that money we've spent on dental care."

"Hi, you must be Carrie. I'm Joel's granddad. I've heard a lot about you – and I saw the video of you on YouTube before it was taken down."

"Well, yes, your boyfriend certainly is a fair bit older than you, dear. But at least he and your granddad will have plenty to talk about."

"So you expect me to believe that you and your boyfriend are living together, sleeping together in the same bed, but you're not having sex? Oh my God! You're not married, are you?"

"Look, boy, don't be railroaded into getting married. Nobody's forcing you, not in this day and age. It was different for your grandma and me – we *had* to get married, if you get my drift. Maybe I shouldn't be telling you this. Not a word to your father."

"Why do you want to get married? There's no need. Getting married is like buying the whole farm just for a bowl of cornflakes."

"So you want a really big wedding with a carriage and horses, a church choir, a huge marquee and all the trimmings? I just want to let you know that your mother and I won't be in the least bit offended if you and Jeremy decide to elope instead."

"Why do you need to hire the services of a wedding

planner? You're staging a simple marriage between two people with a few guests, not the summer Olympics."

"You can always tell on the wedding day whether a marriage is going to last. Like if she stabs with you the knife you've just used to cut the cake – that's never a good sign."

"If you and Brenda are signing one of those pre-nuptial agreements, I just wanted to let you know that your mother and I wouldn't mind getting that coffeemaker back."

"You have the most beautiful eyelashes for a boy. I know you're only eight and you probably haven't given much thought to such matters, but with looks like yours you could grow up to be a real gay icon."

"David, I'm not trying to put you off being gay or anything – but I'm your mother and I just think you ought to know, anal sex really hurts."

"So you're not gay? Thank God! I had a bet with your mother about it and I've won thirty bucks."

"There are only two kinds of men that wear earrings – poofs and pirates. And I don't see a ship out on the drive."

"What do you mean you're bisexual? You can't be. You've never been one for sharing."

"What sort of girl doesn't carry a handbag? You're not a lesbian, are you?"

"You're pretty old to be single, Rachel. Have you thought about becoming one of those lesbians?"

"So what if she prefers girls to boys? Some people prefer horses to dogs. I'd rather live with a lesbian than a horse."

"I can think of worse things in life than being a lesbian. For a start, you wouldn't have to cook a full dinner every day if you didn't feel like it."

"It's not all bad news. At least being a lesbian you won't get knocked up."

"I tell all my friends how great it is having a lesbian daughter. You get all the hunting trips and beer drinking of a son but none of the worry that she'll impregnate some random slapper."

"Waiter, this is my grandson, Justin. He's gay. I don't suppose you have any eligible gay friends that he might be able to hook up with – ideally a doctor or a lawyer?"

"Listen, some people are just born gay, the same as some people are born with big noses. That's the way it is. So don't let anyone give you shit for being gay. Okay? And don't let anyone give you shit about your big nose either."

"Why would you want to be gay, son? There are so many

beautiful women out there – and not even your brother has slept with all of them."

"What am I supposed to tell my friends at the coffee morning? That you have a lady husband – that my son-in-law Gerald now prefers to be known as my daughter-in-law Geraldine? And you think you can stay married? What's going to happen the first time you go out together and find that you're wearing identical dresses? Have you thought about that, the embarrassment?"

# 7

# Don't Give Me Any of This Technology Shit

*Old people and new technology generally mix about as well as oil and water. Twitter gives them the jitters, they can't tell an Xbox from a fuse box, and many still can't understand why the postman never brings them any emails. Like twenty-first century Luddites, they see these gadgets as the enemy, designed solely for young, nimble fingers instead of arthritic joints. It makes them feel excluded, redundant and worthless, so when in the company of young people they retaliate in the only way they know how – by bringing out dusty old photo albums and a jigsaw puzzle.*

"You kids and your damn tripods! Turn them off and listen to me!"

"I have twelve CDs. I listen to eight of them. I like four of them. Why the fuck would I need something that holds 30,000 songs?"

"So you can listen to music on your iPod all day long if you like? We used to have something like that when I was a teenager. We called it the radio."

"Yeah, it sure is slim – slim enough to slip down the side of the sofa and not be found for six months."

"You don't know the meaning of the word? Why don't you go look it up on your fancy earpod?"

"I can't read the screen on this goddam phone without my glasses. I keep getting messages or missed calls from someone called Betty Low . . . Oh, right . . . Battery low."

"Stop playing with your phone, dumbass. It's not your pecker."

"Why would I want a mobile phone that takes photos? If I want to take a photo, I use a camera. If I want to make a phone call, I use a phone. Simple as that. After all, if I wanted to make a cup of tea, I wouldn't use an electric razor."

"It's a mobile phone. What do you mean, what does it do? It makes a phone call when I press the button. What do you expect it to do? Mow the lawn? Cook a three-course meal? Fuck your mother?"

"What's the point of missed calls? If I'd wanted to speak to that person, I'd have answered the bloody phone. Instead, I get a bloody message telling me to speak to somebody I didn't want to talk to in the first place."

"Why would I take my phone with me? I'm only going to the newspaper shop – a journey of, oh, 500 yards. I'm hardly likely to get abducted by aliens on the way. My phone and I are not attached at the hip. Unlike your generation I don't take it into the bathroom with me every time I take a shit. What do you do with it in there anyway – send a photo of your dump to your friends? Check out the bits of sweetcorn. LOL."

"People can't even move around the house without taking their mobile phone with them. There's no respite. Having a mobile phone is the technological equivalent of a woman lying on the bed with her legs wide open all the time."

"Has anyone ever told you that you look like a total dickhead with that fancy Bluetooth headset? You're not the Chief Communications Officer of the Starship *Enterprise* – you're a waiter in a coffee bar asking your mother if you can bring over your laundry."

"Bluetooth, huh? It's about the only thing I haven't been treated for in the past twelve months."

"So you've lost your phone?! What do you expect me to do – wear black for a month? It's not like you've lost an arm or a leg. All it will have on it are a few shaky photos and some phone numbers that you've got written down in an address book anyway. Life's tough, so I guess you'll just have to survive for a few days without knowing what the weather's like in Buenos Aires."

"Why the fuck have you got a ringtone that plays 'The Birdie Song'? Is it because you're worried there are still one or two people out there who don't know that you're a knobhead?"

"By the way, thanks for the text message. I have no idea what it said because there were no recognizable words. But thanks anyway."

"Aren't you a bit old to be using text message abbreviations? I thought it was strictly for kids. You're forty-four. Isn't it something you should have grown out of by now like Disney movies and wetting the bed?"

"I can't get the hang of this texting lark. My fingers can't get into tight spaces any more. Isn't that right, Mildred?"

"Predictive text? What the fuck's that? How can the phone know what word I want to write when I don't even know?"

"Your grandma's just texted me to say she's hung her tits

out to dry. I think she may have accidentally pressed the 't' instead of the 'b'."

"I can never read the damn letters on my mobile phone. The writing's too small, and that's how mistakes occur. Last week I texted your father and told him I'd made him a nice crap sandwich for lunch. He didn't rush home."

"How come my sixteen-year-old granddaughter receives over sixty text messages a day while I'm lucky if I get one a week – and that's from the phone company? Why is she so much more popular than I am? Is there something that people aren't telling me? Do I need to start showering more often?"

"I left your DVD on the table, George, but I can't figure out how to rewind it."

"It took me twenty-five years to figure out how to programme the video recorder, and when I finally cracked it, everything switched to DVD. So I reckon I'll be in that great Sony showroom in the sky long before I figure out how to programme the DVD recorder."

"How am I supposed to get this bastard machine to work when half of the handbook is written in a foreign language?"

"So your newfangled TV has got thirty-five channels, including no fewer than four different shopping channels? I can see how that would be impossible to resist. After all, what better way of wasting your life than gazing at some bimbo caressing a potato peeler as if it were her boyfriend's dick?"

"I don't want to watch boring old cookery programmes at my age, not when there's a good murder on another channel."

"Apart from the Adult Movie Channel, there's just nothing for us old people to watch on TV any more."

"You know that they call the Weather Channel? Old folks' MTV."

"We've gone digital – but only because your father can no longer get an erection."

"You say with HD TV it'll be almost like having the people on screen in my own front room? That's all very well, but the day I find Simon Cowell in my front room is the day I move house."

"So with a 3D picture they virtually jump out of the screen at you? Hmm, I'm not sure about getting one. I'm worried that it will further confuse your grandma who's convinced that everyone on screen is hiding in the back of the set anyway."

"You can talk to the people on the TV all you want, but I can almost guarantee you that Huw Edwards won't say, 'Goodnight, Mildred,' at the end of reading the news bulletin."

"That's why they call it a remote, Mildred – because you never have the remotest idea where the fucking thing is."

"Darling, I think the batteries must have gone in this remote thingy because I can't get it to change channels . . . Oh, it's a mobile phone, is it? Well, how was I to know – these blasted gadgets all look the same to me."

"Were you born dumb? You go out and spend all that money on some newfangled digital camera, but you forget to buy a fucking film for it!"

"So all I have to do is press 'Send', and the fax message goes to the right person? And you're absolutely sure I don't have to put a stamp on it?"

"Why waste all that money on expensive gadgets? Are all these things really necessary? Remember, you don't need a parachute to skydive. You only need a parachute to skydive twice."

"At my age, my reclining chair has more gadgets than my car."

"You say it's a reclining chair that you plug in? So basically you bought your old man an electric chair. Thanks for nothing, son."

"Why do they say something's 'new and improved'? Which is it? If it's new, then there has never been anything before it. If it's an improvement, then there must have been something before it."

"Blackberry, blueberry, raspberry, it's all the same to me. All I know is it's something I can do without at my time of life, like fuel bills and piles."

"Don't blind me with all this modern technology. The only gadget I need at my time of life is the dimmer switch."

"Never mind about an iPad, your father still doesn't know how to use the iRon."

"Do I want to see your Wii? Why not? It makes a change from mopping up your grandma's."

"So this Wii tennis game is supposed to be just like the real thing? Except that it takes place in your living room, and you don't actually get to hit a ball – and on Centre Court you don't have to worry about tripping over the cat or knocking over a vase of flowers. I guess I'll just have to use my imagination."

"It's time you came off of that damn computer. You've been on it for long enough. It's not good for you. Come and watch some TV."

"How should I know what the capital of Kazakhstan is? Why don't you look it up on your fucking Google machine?"

"Do you have Google where you live?"

"Don't interrupt me – I'm on the Google."

"So you think 'asswipe' would be an appropriate password for me, do you, son? You obviously haven't given much thought to your inheritance lately, have you?"

"Why do they call it 'surfing' the net, as if it's some kind of athletic pursuit? It's not surfing at all – it's just bloody typing in your bedroom."

"Well, I happen to think the Internet is really educational and useful – and not just for the porn."

"There's so much you can learn from the Internet. How else would I have found out how to contact sexy Eastern European girls in my neighbourhood?"

"No, I don't want to play poker online again. It's like being mugged but without the company."

"I'm sure it brings a great deal of pleasure to the feeble-minded but I just can't conceive how boring my life would have to be to make me want to sign up with Twitter."

"Why would I want to join Twitter? I'm an old man. I ramble. I can't tell you what day it is in fewer than 140 characters."

"Britney Spears has got over six million followers on Twitter? That's six million people who need to get a life."

"And you've got over a hundred followers on Twitter, have you? Sounds impressive, but it still doesn't make you fucking Jesus."

"I've just managed to pull out a particularly long nose-hair that I've been after for days. Tweet that to your disciples."

"I've just been upstairs on the computer and somebody poked me. What should I do? I feel quite giddy."

"Don't give me all that stuff about how great Facebook is. When are you going to realize that the people who sign on to your page are no more your friends than your right hand is your girlfriend?"

"My computer screen says I've performed an illegal action, but I haven't done anything wrong. Will I have to go to jail?"

"I had a message pop up on a website this morning with something about cookies . . . Which website was it? Uh, let me think . . . Betty Crocker's."

"I've been trying to explain to your father that just because he's got online banking doesn't mean he can click a button to make ten-pound notes come out of the hard drive."

"How come this computer's so slow? I got more bytes than this the last time I went fishing."

"What speed has my computer got? Depends on how hard I throw the damn thing out of the window."

"Are you really surprised that the camera you ordered online never arrived? I said to you at the time that the website looked dodgy – no phone number, no proper address, no secure payment page. You might as well have paid your dough to youvebeenshafted.com."

"So you say I can send Aunt Maisie the link by copying and pasting it into the send box? How am I supposed to copy and paste the Internet? Are you trying to trick me?"

"Mildred, what should I do? The computer says my recycle bin's full, and I know the men don't come until Wednesday."

"Yes, I know it says you're the 10,000th visitor to that site and that you've won a prize. But I wouldn't hand in your notice at work just yet . . . Why not? Try looking up the word 'gullible' in the dictionary."

"The Internet's a curse. Mrs Johnson at number 63 split up with her husband because she started getting emails about penis enlargement and realized what she'd been missing out on all these years."

"Your grandma walked out on me after I blew our life savings on one of these penis extensions. She said she couldn't take it any longer."

"I'm not sure about all this electronic mail. I prefer regular mail. It's the same with an ordinary chair and an electric chair – I know which one I'd rather sit in."

"The computer says I've got mail, so I'm just going out front to fetch it."

"Don't send me that email yet. My computer isn't switched on, so I won't receive it."

# 8

# It's The Way I Talk – If You Don't Like It, Go Boil Your Head

*Old people are forever complaining that youngsters talk in a language all of their own, but they seem to forget that there is an equally impenetrable geriatric dictionary full of words like "whippersnapper", "flabbergasted", "highfalutin", "whoops-a-daisy" and "poppycock" plus phrases such as "not the foggiest", "as bent as a donkey's hind leg" and the classic "well, I'll go to the foot of our stairs". So they see no irony in demanding of their teenage grandson: "What in tarnation does 'minging' mean?" Above all, old people should never attempt yoofspeak. "Wicked" should only be used to refer to murderers, "cool" should only describe the contents of the refrigerator and "hip" should only be used when prefixed by "artificial".*

"Where am I going? I'm going to the bathroom. I'm gonna water the horse. Wanna hold its head?"

"I won't be long. I'm just going to point Percy at the porcelain . . . shake the dew off the lily. . .shake hands with the president."

"Stop bouncin' around like a fart on a grill."

"Drop your cocks and grab your socks. It's time to get up."

"I gotta piss like a two-peckered billygoat!"

"Well, I'll be dipped in shit and rolled in cornflakes!"

"Well, butter my bum and call me a biscuit!"

"She might not be the prettiest woman on this Earth, but you don't look at the mantelpiece when you're poking the fire."

"Why fart and waste it when you can burp and taste it?"

"I'm so hungover, I feel like a billygoat ate me and shat me off a cliff."

"You're hungover. Your eyes look like two piss-holes in the snow."

"Who you callin' honey? Do I look like bees' shit to you?"

"Whoever invented decorating wants fucking. Then again whoever invented fucking wants decorating."

"It was so crowded in that room that you couldn't cuss the cat without getting fur in your mouth."

"It's so flat around here, you could stand on a milk crate and watch your dog run away for three days."

"His pants were so tight that if he farted, he'd blow his boots off."

"The only way those jeans weren't too tight is if she'd got shot in the backside and was trying to stop the bleeding."

"If only, if only, if only . . . What's the point of saying 'if only'? If my aunt had balls she'd be my uncle!"

"If your nose runs and your feet smell, then God built you upside down."

"Well, dip my balls in sweet cream and squat me in a kitchen full of kittens!"

"I'm so hungry I could eat the balls off a low-flying duck."

"I'm so hungry my belly button is sticking out of my backside."

"It's like trying to get fly shit off a pinhead with boxing gloves on."

"It's darker in here than in the inside of a cow."

"That boy was shakin' like a dog shittin' razor blades."

"I'm more tired than a one-armed well-digger."

"I feel as tired as a cucumber in a convent."

"He's so scared you couldn't drive a wet watermelon seed up his butt with a sledgehammer."

"He's busier than a cat covering up shit on a concrete floor."

"Mark my words, that boy's nuttier than a squirrel turd."

"I'm hornier than a nine-dicked dog in a kennel full of bitches."

"Which woman is prettier? I dunno. It's harder to pick than a broken nose."

"That guy over there is uglier than the east end of a horse headed west."

"He looks like something the dog's been keepin' under the porch."

"She's so ugly she would make a buzzard back off from a bucket of guts."

"If my dog was as ugly as her, I'd shave his ass and teach him to walk backwards."

"She's so ugly her feet wouldn't go to bed with her."

"I wouldn't say she's ugly but I wouldn't fuck her with your dick."

"That woman is so ugly she could eat corn through a picket fence."

"She's so ugly she makes onions cry."

"Ugly tree, my ass! That girl ran through the ugly forest and never missed a branch."

"What are you going to use for a face when the baboon wants his ass back?"

"She's wound up tighter than the girdle of a Baptist minister's wife at an all-you-can-eat pancake breakfast."

"Show me a man who has both feet on the ground, and I'll show you a man who can't put on his pants."

"So you don't know who the father is? Well, when you go through a briar patch, you don't know which briar scratched you."

"That book is older than your grandma, and she's so old she farts dust."

"Do I want another drink? What do you think? Does a bear shit in the woods?"

"Would I like to come back to your place? Does a fat baby fart?"

"Would I like the chance of winning a million pounds? Does a one-legged duck swim in circles?"

"When you're up to your ass in alligators, it's hard to remember that you came to drain the swamp."

"Cough it up, boy. It might be a gold watch."

"It's not the cough that carries you off, it's the coffin they carry you off in."

"You go right ahead and do that if you want. Whatever cranks your tractor."

"I'm wasting my time talking to you. I may as well be shovelling shit from China."

"I'm hangin' in there like loose teeth."

"It's better to be pissed at and missed than shit at and hit."

"I didn't know whether to shit or go blind, so I closed one eye and farted."

"That job was tougher than trying to put butter up a wild cat's backside with a hot poker."

"She's so clumsy she could trip over a cordless phone."

"That boy's more slippery than snot on a glass doorknob."

"He's as slick as cat shit on linoleum."

"He's more slippery than two eels fuckin' in a bucket of snot."

"Well, don't you look prettier than a glob of butter melting on a stack of wheat cakes!"

"He's happier than a pig in shit."

"I ain't had this much fun since the hogs ate your sister."

"I'm having more fun than a tornado in a trailer park."

"Well, fuck me red raw!"

"Hear that thunder and lightning? It's a good night for a murder."

"Don't you piss on my leg and tell me it's rainin'!"

"It's raining like a cow pissing on a flat rock."

"It's been so long since it rained, I saw two trees fighting over a hound dog."

"It's drier than Happy Hour at the Betty Ford clinic."

"It's drier than a dead dingo's donger."

"It's hotter than two squirrels fucking in a wool sock."

"It's hotter than a donkey's ass in a pepper patch."

"I'm sweatin' like a whore in church on a Sunday."

"It's so cold out that the guy on the newsstand who gives me the finger every day was wearing mittens and said I'd have to take his word for it."

"It's colder than a witch's tit in a tin bra."

"It's colder than a mother-in-law's kiss."

"It's cold enough to freeze the balls off a brass monkey."

"It's cold enough to freeze the balls off a pool table."

"It's so cold here we've got dogs stuck to fire hydrants all over town."

"Well, stick a paper umbrella up my butt and call me a hurricane!"

"Tell me something: why do some folks say: 'You can't have your cake and eat it too'? What's the point of a cake you can't eat?"

"Why do people often say they are beside themselves? They don't really mean it. To my mind, you can only be beside yourself if you are a Siamese twin or a time traveller."

"Why do people ask, 'Can I *borrow* a piece of paper?' Sure, but please don't return the favour! It's one goddamn piece of paper!"

"When you're waiting for the bus, why does someone ask: 'Has the bus come yet?' If the bus had come, I wouldn't be standing here, would I?"

"Why do people come up to you on the bus, eye the empty seat next to you and then say: 'Is anyone sitting here?' Sure, it's the Invisible Man. Can't you see him?"

"And in bars why do people say to you: 'Is this seat free?' No, it's five dollars an hour – pay up or find some place else to sit!"

"Why do people say: 'Can I ask you a question?' Didn't really give me much of a choice there, did you, my friend?"

"Why do they call some cars 'people carriers'? Aren't all cars people carriers?"

"Why do they call them 'safety matches'? What's safe about something that could burn your house down?"

"Why do I take God's name in vain when I swear? Listen, if he wants all the credit for the good things in life then he's got to take all the blame when shit happens."

# 9

# Bloody Kids!

*Other than a weak bladder and dentures that don't fit properly, the biggest source of frustration and irritation for old people is their own children. The older generation have set such high standards of decorum that they just can't understand why the snivelling little motherfuckers can't match them. Instead, kids are ungrateful, selfish and not even interested in old John Wayne movies. Still, it's nothing that a damn good beating won't cure. That'll earn some respect.*

"Don't marry your own cousin – you'll end up with the type of kids your mother and I had."

"Kids. Can't live with them, can't shoot them."

"Is it too much to fucking ask that you show some manners at the dinner table?"

"Isn't it about time you had kids? You think we raised you so you could enjoy your thirties? It's time for you to deal with the shit and the diapers and for us to have some fun."

"Look at the state of you! Your hair's a mess, you need a shave, and you smell like a zoo. In fact, I remember once driving past a zoo in Germany and it smelt just like you do."

"Damn kids today! Floggin's too good for 'em. But hangin', drawin' and quarterin' isn't."

"I never said you wouldn't amount to much! I said you wouldn't amount to anything!"

"You know, son, there are times when I think you must have sneaked into the gene pool when the lifeguard wasn't looking."

"You've got something on your mind? Well, I'm glad to hear it because there was me thinking the only time you ever had anything on your mind was when you wore a hat!"

"When I compare you to your hard-working sister, all I know is if I were a bird, I know which one I'd shit on first."

"Just imagine how much smarter you'd be if I hadn't knocked back three bottles of wine a week when I was pregnant with you."

"I pushed you out of my vagina but you're too damn lazy to make a phone call and tell me you're staying over at a friend's!"

"No, Kelly, you can't have the last slice of apple pie. So stop asking. I gave you life, now leave me alone."

"I brought you into this world and I can damn well take you out again!"

"Sure I've paid for sex. From the very minute you were born . . ."

"Even as a child you were a disappointment. Cyril Brown's boy got to play Joseph in the school nativity play. I know not every kid can play Joseph but at least if you'd have been the innkeeper I could have shown my face at the golf club again. But no, not you; you weren't even a shepherd – you were a bloody donkey who just stood around in a corner of the stable looking at his watch."

"That must be your ass talking, son, because surely by now your mouth knows better."

"Some days I look at you and say to myself: 'Was she really worth getting stretch marks for?' "

"So you let me win at golf? What did you have to go and tell me that for? The one time in your life you do something decent, you have to spoil it by opening your big mouth. Couldn't you just have let me go quietly to my grave with a little pride, a little dignity from the knowledge that once, just once, I'd whipped my son's fucking ass at golf?"

"You want to go ice skating on the lake? Wait till it gets warmer."

"You think you're focused at work? I'll tell you how focused you are most of the day – you're about as focused as a fart."

"I hope you do pass your work exam, but I gotta say there have been times when I didn't think you were capable of passing water."

"I didn't spend a small fortune on getting you privately educated just so that you could say every day: 'Do you want fries with that?' "

"So you've got ambition? What's that supposed to prove? A fly's got ambitions to get out of the room, but it still keeps banging its head against the window."

"When it comes to skills in the office, you're not even a one-trick pony. You're a pony that just stands around all day eating and shits where the other ponies are trying to work."

"Yeah, I reckon you've got a chance of getting promoted at work. And look, there goes another flying pig."

"I'll tell you why your mother and I never divorced – because neither of us wanted custody of you."

"Sure I'll keep you in the loop – in fact I'll make sure your head never slips out of the noose."

"Sometimes, son, I think you are the reason God created the middle finger."

"You spend all day in bed, and then you're out all night. If you didn't like garlic, I'd be seriously worried about you."

"You ungrateful little twat! You just don't appreciate the

sacrifices I made for you. I'll have you know I left a ball game fifteen minutes before the end to attend your birth, and I didn't catch all of the reruns on the TV at the hospital."

"Son, the last thing I want to do is hurt you, but it's still on the list."

"There's something I like about you, son. Give me a couple of months and I'll remember it."

"Why couldn't you have been like other kids and got pregnant at sixteen? I miss having babies around the house."

"I'm sick of you boys fighting all the time. Go out the back, slug it out, and the first one to cry is grounded."

"You and your brother are going to arm wrestle each other? What's that going to prove? All it will show is which of you is the biggest wanker."

"I guess I'm glad we had two sons instead of two daughters. That way I was only ever worried about two dicks in town instead of every dick in town."

"If you give birth to two daughters, drown one."

"Aren't you too old to be playing soccer in the street? Shouldn't you be doing drugs instead?"

"You're off to a *Star Trek* convention in Minneapolis? You didn't exactly turn out to be Mr Cool, did you, son?"

"You were never exactly a typical student, were you? I remember that time your flatmates went off to an all-night party carrying crates of booze but you decided to stay at home to repair a hole in your washing-up gloves."

"Football's a contact sport, son, so sure you're going to get kicked from time to time. If you want something less physical, take up knitting . . . again."

"When are you going to tidy your room? It smells like a ghetto apartment block . . . Okay, wise guy, so two days ago I said it smelled like a crack house. I was trying to be politically correct back then."

"Too bad children aren't like waffles. You should be able to throw the first one out."

"I try to be proud of you, son. Really I try. Just like Mrs Hitler must have tried."

"They say that when you're born, you get a ticket to the freak show. I guess that with you for a son I've got a front-row seat."

"You've got a birthday card from your grandparents . . . Which ones? The ones that are still alive, dickhead!"

"Boy, has nobody ever told you that you should never drink on an empty head?"

"I knew we should have had chickens instead of kids. We could have killed them and eaten them."

"Buck up your ways or we're going to fall out big time. I can still sell you to the gypsies."

"I can get rid of you anytime I choose. I know how to make another one just like you."

"Do you know what they call you at the construction site? Blister, they call you Blister. You want to know why? Because you don't show up until the work is finished."

"If you don't mind, I'd like to finish reading the paper first. Poor planning and lack of forethought on your part do not constitute an emergency on my part."

"Tell me something, boy: were you born stupid or have you just practised hard?"

"He's gone out, left the refrigerator door open and the food inside has started to go off. Looks like we've had another visit from the fuck-up fairy."

"For a fleeting moment there, I thought you were talking sense. It must be time to up my medication."

"Sometimes, son, you make about as much sense as wiping before you poop."

"You talk so much bollocks that I think you must have had your head down there taking language lessons from the pair of them."

"You're so full of shit, you're nothing more than a bowel with hair."

"Why don't you try agreeing with me? For once in your life you might find out what it feels like to be right."

"You want to borrow how much?! Are you for real, son? Or are you just visiting this planet?"

"Why would I want to let you borrow my credit card even for a day? I'd rather stand in a urinal next to Shakin' Stevens."

"You want an allowance? You've already got an allowance. I allow you to live in my house, I allow you to eat my food and I allow you to sit on furniture that I've bought. Now go out and cut the grass."

"If I do agree to lend you my credit card, I don't want you using it to pay for a hooker. Hookers are strictly cash only."

"Let me get this straight: you want me to pay a subscription so that you can listen to music on the TV? What the fuck's wrong with the radio?"

"So you think you'd like to sail around the world? You keep thinking, son – it's what you're good at."

"The plan is simple, son, just like you. But unlike you, the plan might just work."

"Don't shake your head like there's nothing in it."

"Don't you have a mind of your own? If everyone else was on fire, would you set yourself alight too?"

"You're worried about identity fraud? Get real, son. Who the hell would want to steal your identity? That wino who sleeps rough and talks to the pigeons in the park wouldn't want to swap places with you!"

"You're not sure whether to wear the blue shirt or the black shirt? Try to imagine how little I care."

"Son, are you taking part in some experiment to determine whether humans can function without a brain?"

"Is something wrong with you? Are you going through some kind of nonentity crisis?"

"I don't get all this modern psychobabble. You think you've got self-esteem issues because you reckon you're a worthless individual? Does that mean that your mother, your sister and me have the same issues because we all reckon you're a worthless individual, too?"

"So you're planning on leaving your body to science, eh? Well, it wouldn't surprise me if science contests the will."

"Shut that goddamn door. Do you want to heat the whole town?"

"How much fucking longer are you going to be in that bathroom? Either shit your lot or get off the pot."

"As long as you're living under my roof, you'll abide by my rules – and they include not taking the last biscuit."

"Shut your mouth and eat your dinner."

"If you don't behave, I'll unscrew your belly button and your backside will fall off."

"Boy, you'd rather run through fire with gasoline drawers on than fuck with me!"

"If you weren't thirty-eight and I didn't have a bad back, I'd put you over my knee and give you a damn good hiding!"

"First you were a pain in my vagina and now you're a pain in my ass!"

"I wanted you to be raised as a Catholic, but I lost that argument. I was also in favour of abortion but I lost that argument, too."

"You're a mistake, boy – you're nothing but a torn condom!"

"Did you know that one in every three people is suffering from some form of mental illness? Your mother and I are okay, so it must be you."

"Boy, you could fuck up a wet dream!"

"Son, you're so full of shit, it's coming out your ears."

"I don't want to take you fishing. That's the whole point of the exercise – I go by myself so that I can get some peace and quiet for a day. Just me, the river and the fish. Hell, the only way I'd ever contemplate taking you fishing is if I could use you as bait!"

"Of course I remember you as a baby. You were like a little angel sent down from heaven to fuck up my life."

"She's our granddaughter! Sure she's a two-timing whore, but she's our two-timing whore."

"Your grandpa and me were both convinced you'd grow up to be a hooker."

"All I ever wanted was one gay son. Just one. That's not too much to ask, is it?"

"You must have a secret twin we don't know about because I don't think it's possible to get this much disappointment from one fucking son."

"You told me you were going to take up sport, be a champion, make me proud. Instead, you've taken up swimming. Swimming's not a sport – it's something you do to keep from drowning."

"You know, when I look at you and think of what you've done with your life – no job, no girlfriend, still living with your folks at the age of thirty-seven – I say to myself: son, you should have been a blow job."

# 10

# I May Be Old, But I've Still Got Lead in My Pencil

*A common misconception among youngsters is that people stop having sex when they reach the age of sixty. In fact, free from the stresses of bringing up kids, perky pensioners make the average rabbit look celibate. Furthermore, they have no inhibitions and are almost impossible to embarrass, even in the event of having to be prised apart by fire crews after ageing joints meant they were unable to extricate themselves while attempting to recreate figure 118 in* The Joy of Sex. *Well, it was something to tell their friends about at the next bridge evening.*

"Put your teeth in, gorgeous – you've pulled."

"You want to know why sex with your mother is still so good even in our eighties? It's because every time we do it, we think it could be the last time."

"I didn't lose my virginity until I was twenty-nine. Eighteen vaginally, but twenty-nine what your grandpa calls 'the real way'."

"When we were courting, your father and I lived twenty miles apart, but he still came over three times a week in his car. It was what he called his sex drive."

"I don't know when my tits started to sag like this. Thank God I won't live another ten years or they'll be down to my knees."

"If you're going to have a fucking tattoo, get eyeballs on the bottom of your boobs so when you get old and saggy like me you can fling them over your shoulder and scare the hell out of the neighbourhood kids."

"Nowadays all I have to do to see your mother's tits is ask her to lift up her skirt."

"It's so tough getting a job once you're in your sixties. I'm that desperate for work, I'd apply for a job at Hooters if I wasn't so flat chested."

"Come on, be honest with me. Do you think seventy-nine is too old to have a boob job?"

"Bert from the bowling club took Viagra and now he's insatiable. Seventy-seven years old and he's got women queuing up for his services. He's killed off three members of the team in the last six months alone."

"Your grandpa's getting some of that Viagra from the doctor so we can start having sex again. It means I can finally stop thinking about that young man who came to repair our boiler in 1998."

"I don't take Viagra because I'm impotent – I take it

because old women are so goddamn ugly!"

"Not that it's any of your business, but despite 'having one foot in the grave' as you put it, your father and I still have regular sex. And he doesn't need Viagra to get it up!"

"I remember when we were younger, your father and I once made love for one hour and two minutes. Mind you, it was the night the clocks were put forward."

"Did I ever tell you about the time just after the war when your mother and I went to make love in a field? I was twenty-one, she was eighteen. She looked so beautiful as she lay naked on the grass next to me. I learned a lot that day – like in future how to recognize an ants' nest."

"Your father loves the hot summer days. They make him feel randy; it's his rutting season."

"I'm so horny, even the crack of dawn ain't safe."

"I would drag my bare balls over ten miles of broken glass just to finger fuck her shadow."

"Your father doesn't buy that type of magazine any more, not because he's become prudish but with his bad back he can no longer reach up to the top shelf."

"If I'd known about oral sex before I got married, I'd never have got married."

"If you do oral sex, does it count against your weight watchers points?"

"I'll tell you the worst thing about oral sex: the view."

"Last week I was licking clotted cream off your father's dick, and I suddenly thought: 'Oh my God, I'm turning into my mother!'"

"Why won't I give head? Because I don't believe it is God's

will. If God had intended women to give oral sex, he would have made sperm taste like chocolate."

"George, meet Pedro. You always said you wondered what I'd look like with a Brazilian."

"Your mother went from a size B to a size C after having you two, so for that I thank you."

"Why did I smack the nurse across her backside? Because it was big and it was there."

"You know what they say is the best exercise when you get older? Sex and swimming. And you don't see me going to the pool."

"I like a woman's legs to be like peanut butter – tan, smooth, and easy to spread."

"Even though I'm seventy-six, I still use a condom when I

have sex, because I can't stand the damp."

"If you ever need any condoms, don't be shy. Just ask your father – he's got plenty. In fact, he's still got five in the packet of six I bought him last Christmas."

"I found these old condoms in my drawer, boy. Do you want them? Now that your grandma and I are in our eighties I feel like living dangerously."

"When it comes to sex nowadays there's a lot of pressure on men to be in the driving seat – especially on a dogging night."

"At our age your mother and I prefer threesomes – in case one of us dies."

"I'm sorry your father's in a bad mood, but I'm having a really heavy period and he's getting frustrated."

"Sure I can multitask, Mildred. You just never caught me jacking off while I was looking at *Baywatch*."

"Don't knock masturbation, son. There's a lot to be said for it. There's no pressure for a start. If you're jacking off and nothing happens, it remains a secret between you and the paper tissue – you don't have to reassure the tissue that it wasn't to blame and that the fluid failure was probably due to stress at work. Nor do you feel obliged to make the tissue feel fulfilled. You just crumple it up in your back pocket and try again later."

"I read in the paper that regular masturbation is good for you. Apparently whacking one off on a regular basis can reduce the risk of prostate cancer. That's the kind of medicine I like."

"Have I ever tried bondage? Hell, no – apart from the time my pyjama cord got accidentally wrapped around the bedpost."

"We weren't thought of as sluts in the 1970s because everyone was doing it."

"I may look like a sweet old grandma to you kids, but you know the Grand Old Duke of York who had 10,000 men? Well, I can beat his total with a few platoons to spare."

"Never you mind how old I am, young man! Let's just say I reached the age of consent about 15,000 consents ago."

"I don't mind telling you how old I am. I'm sixty-eight, and have been for the last eleven years."

"For an old 'un, my lower body is still really firm. I reckon I could crack walnuts with my buttocks."

"I don't reckon I'm in bad shape for a grandma of seventy-six. I think I could be a GILF."

"Sex at my age is still great – even though each year it becomes harder to see who I'm having it with."

"I'm not too old to pick up women. Last week I met a woman, took her back to my place and we did it doggy style – not because we planned it that way, but that's just how she passed out."

"If you happen to be passing that new pole-dancing club on London Road, will you ask them if they do senior citizens' discounts?"

"I'm not past it yet. I still get admiring glances down at the bar, and when men ask how old I am, I tell them I'm sixty-five plus VAT."

"Lady, your dog's been humping my leg. You may say he's just being friendly, but if I went over to you – a complete stranger – and started humping you, would you accept my explanation that I was just being friendly? I don't think so."

"I wouldn't make any calls just yet. Your father had phone sex last night, and I haven't got round to cleaning the receiver."

"Your father happily pays £2.50 a minute to talk to a woman in Thailand about mutual orgasms, yet he moans about having to pay 20 pence a minute to talk to a woman in India from Mutual Insurance."

"I remember your father proposing to me at school. In fact, I can still recall his actual words – 'You're having a what?!' "

"When we were first married, your father and I used to fight like cat and dog. I remember that to stop him leaving me one day, I hid his truck key in my vagina. The funny thing is I don't ever recall taking it out again."

"I guess celebrating our fiftieth wedding anniversary is quite an occasion. I mean, not even a gopher stays in the same hole fifty years!"

"Your son is a seriously good-looking kid. I tell you, if I was fifty years younger I'd be all over him like a rash."

"What do you mean, do I practise safe sex? Safe sex for me these days means not falling out of bed."

"Sex at eighty-two is still a wonderful experience – especially the one in the winter."

"Your grandma and me don't bother much with sex these days. Once she used to give head, now she gives headache."

"Sex with your mother at eighty is like throwing a cane into a dusty corner."

"George, I wish you would grow up. I don't like it when you stand naked at the foot of the bed like that."

"When you get to ninety, having sex is like trying to shoot pool with a rope."

"So what if my zipper's undone? At my age it doesn't matter. A dead bird doesn't leave the nest."

"What do I want with a condom? At my age all I'm concerned about on a date is remembering to put my teeth in and putting on reasonably clean underpants."

"I'm afraid the only pop-ups your father gets these days are on the computer."

"And the only thing that goes down on me is my computer."

"I always think of your father in bed as being like an umbrella. Not because he protects me, but because he stops me getting wet."

"Your mother's streaking days are over. The last time she tried was at a flower show and she won a prize for Best Dried Arrangement."

"Sure, I used to have all-nighters when I was young. But at my age an 'all-nighter' means not having to get up to pee."

"You kind of lose interest in sex when you get to my age. You know what I mean, it's difficult to get aroused? The last time I got my dick out, your mother took one look at it and said: 'Does it need watering?' "

"A joke's a joke."

"A poke's a poke."

"But no poke is no joke."

# 11

# Don't Trust The Commie Bastards – Or Anyone Else For That Matter

*Old people are naturally suspicious. Tell them a "knock knock" joke and they'll insist on seeing your ID before replying. They pride themselves on being shrewd judges of character. Miss Marple could always spot a wrong 'un several chapters before the local constabulary, while any number of Jessica Fletcher's nieces and nephews would still be languishing behind bars to this day were it not for their aunt's uncanny knack of being able to unmask a murderer. So when a granny says that someone can't be trusted because one nostril is wider than the other, take heed.*

"Never trust a man who doesn't think a fart is funny."

"Never trust men with beards. They have something to hide."

"Never trust a man with short legs. His brain is too near his ass."

"Never trust a man whose tie is lighter than his shirt."

"Never accept a drink from a urologist."

"Never trust a doctor who tries to take your temperature with his finger."

"Never trust a barber with blood on his shirt."

"Never trust a man whose eyebrows meet in the middle. Especially if he's wearing pointy shoes. It just ain't natural."

"Never trust a priest with a boner – and definitely never trust a nun with a boner."

"I told you not to trust that tattoo parlour. The guy clearly didn't know a word of Chinese. So now instead of a Chinese tattoo that says 'I Love Jenny', you've got one saying 'I Fuck Chihuahuas' . . . No, I know it's not my problem. All I'm saying is, don't go near Chinatown."

"Never buy a DVD Recorder in the street from a man who is out of breath."

"Never trust anyone who can keep half a bar of chocolate 'for later'."

"See that red light flashing at the bottom of that plane? That's the Russians taking pictures."

"Never trust an airline where they ask if anyone on board knows how to fly a plane."

"Never trust a man carrying a small dog."

"Never trust anyone who says, 'I'm on your side.' "

"Never trust a man who says he's the boss at home – he probably lies about other things, too."

"Never trust a man with thin lips."

"I don't trust anyone who turns up at my door unannounced, saying he wants to show me the range of goods he has for sale. For all I know he could be about to march me up the stairs and have his wicked way with me. Although with my luck he probably *is* just selling dusters."

"Never trust a politician who kisses a baby. In fact, never trust a politician."

"My old dad always told me this: politicians and diapers

have one thing in common. They should both be changed regularly and for the same reason."

"I don't trust doctors. They're always asking you to take your clothes off. I'm eighty-seven years old, and I'm past that sort of thing."

"I don't trust doctors, either. There's no way I'm letting a complete stranger put his hand up there. Well, not his whole hand, and even then only if he promises to warm it before and marry me after!"

"What do you mean, why don't I trust him? Because he's a banker. What more reason do I need?"

"I've never trusted banks. You've only got to look at bank managers – shifty eyes, the lot of 'em."

"You expect honesty from a bank manager? Are you kidding me? Honesty among bankers is about as common as rocking-horse shit."

"I don't trust ATMs. For all you know there could be a man hiding in the wall behind the machine waiting to snatch your card the moment you put it in."

"I don't trust Internet banking. There's all this online fraud you hear about. It's too risky for me. I'd rather keep all my money at home in a biscuit tin. You know, the one marked 'Cash'."

"I don't trust that boy. If you ask me, he's a wolf in cheap clothing."

"Never trust anyone whose job title runs to more than four words."

"Never trust anyone with the words 'financial' or 'adviser' in their job title."

"Why is it that if someone tells you there are one billion stars in the universe, you believe them, but if they tell you a wall has wet paint, you touch it to be sure?"

"Never trust anyone who says: 'This hurts me more than you.'"

"Run a department? I wouldn't trust you to run a bath."

"Never trust a man who keeps his hat on indoors. It's a sure sign of a shifty nature."

"Never trust a man who, when left alone in a room with a tea cosy, does not try it on."

"That man can't be trusted. He's fishier than Lady Godiva's saddle."

"I don't trust all these people who keep banging on about climate change and how the end of the world is nigh. I'd like you to explain how me leaving the TV on standby for a couple of hours instead of switching it off at the wall is going to lead to the extinction of the polar bear."

"I've heard all the global warming arguments, and I'm still not convinced. I don't trust the science. Just because we had a few mild winters doesn't mean it's a lasting trend. Your mother sneezed twice yesterday but I'm not about to have her put down."

"Never entrust your life to a surgeon with more than three plasters on his fingers."

"Never trust a plastic surgeon whose favourite artist is Picasso."

"Never trust a stockbroker who's married to a travel agent."

"Never trust a taxi driver who dives down a side street every time he sees a police car."

"Never trust a street vendor who keeps looking over his shoulder."

"Never trust a man with more than one first name. It's greedy, and that's how he'll turn out, too."

"Never trust a man who says: 'Does anyone know you're here?'"

"Never trust a woman whose favourite movie is *Fatal Attraction*."

"Never trust a man who starts twitching uncontrollably and makes excuses not to go out when there's a full moon."

"Don't trust short men. They have short tempers and are often crazy."

"Stay away from drummers, sweetheart. I read that something about them having rhythm makes their sperm stronger."

"Never trust a man with the surname 'Crippen', because bad genes often run in a family."

"Never trust a man who buys his wife lingerie – but only after first trying it on in the shop."

"Never trust a man who collects instruments of medieval torture."

"Never trust a man who spends more than half an hour in the bathroom every morning."

"Never trust an undertaker boyfriend who on your first date asks how tall you are – and if you're not sure produces a tape measure."

"Never trust a boy who kisses with his eyes open. There's something that ain't quite right about that."

"There's something about that guy I don't like. Maybe it's

the KILL tattoo on his forehead and the swastika on his T-shirt. I don't know – just call it intuition."

"Never trust someone who says, 'Trust me.'"

"I can't believe you're going to that bar – it's full of weirdos. At least let me see what you're wearing so I can describe your dead body to the police."

"Never trust a dog to watch your food."

# 12

# Wanna Hear About My Operation?

*Put two or more old ladies together and once they've finished poring over the failings of their respective husbands, the subject will almost certainly turn to health – or rather, bad health. It becomes a contest to see whose rheumatism/piles/bunions give the greatest discomfort and only ends when one delivers the* coup de grâce: *"Well, the doctors say it's a miracle I'm still alive." Old men are little better. After spending a lifetime avoiding the medical profession at all costs, they suddenly feel compelled to discuss their bowel movements with complete strangers.*

"My poor dear husband suffered terrible constipation. I used to help him to go by digging it out with a spoon. But I always kept the spoon separate from the others."

"Relax. Kids swallow quarters all the time. If she craps out two dimes and a nickel, then you can start worrying."

"When I say I'm a regular guy, I mean I take a shit at about the same time every morning."

"Hey, it's 3.30. You know what time that is? Time for my afternoon bowel movement."

"A good shit is one of the great pleasures in life, son. You know how sometimes you do a crap so big that afterwards you feel you've dropped a pants size? Well, the way I feel at the moment I reckon I'm one giant turd away from fitting into my 2004 jeans."

"That feels better. I've just done the biggest evacuation since Dunkirk."

"That curry certainly did the trick. It was like releasing a flock of starlings."

"If your poo floats in the toilet, it means you're not eating properly. I don't want to find any more floaters this week, George – only submarines."

"Big disappointment that one! Just a few pellets and a floater. The two-metre-long brown snake is still in its burrow."

"You don't need to tell me you've done a dump! The fact that I heard you trying to get rid of the smell with the air freshener by spraying away like an old tomcat told me all I needed to know."

"When you're young, you can take a shit whenever you want. You rule your bowels. But let me tell you, when you get older, your bowels rule you."

"I'm going for a shit, and in the words of Captain Oates, I may be some time."

"Where's the Preparation H? If I don't get some in my ass real quick, I'm gonna drag my butt on the ground like a dog."

"I'm a martyr to my bowels. I once went eight days without going to the toilet. It felt like a log jam in a tiny brook."

"There are three things I can't abide in life: cruelty to animals, that Katie Price woman and constipation."

"Your mother will be down in a minute. She's caught between two stools."

"You were a relatively easy birth, sweetheart. No trouble at all. In fact I've had shits that were more painful than having you."

"Mildred, I'm afraid I've just pissed in the shower . . . Yes, of course it was an accident, but these things can happen when you're having a shit."

"Pull over, pull over! I've got to pee so bad I can taste it."

"Even at my age I never have to get up in the middle of the

night to go to the bathroom. My bladder is like clockwork – I always pee first thing in the morning at seven o'clock. It's just a shame I don't wake up till eight."

"Where have I been? Okay, I'll tell you where I've been. Have you ever had an itch that was driving you crazy, but you can't scratch it around everyone? Well, my haemorrhoids have been itching like crazy, so I've just been upstairs scratching the shit out of them. It felt so damn good, it was orgasmic."

"I've just had an operation for piles. All my troubles are behind me."

"These haemorrhoids are a real pain in the neck."

"That wasn't farting. That was pre-pooping."

"No way am I embarrassed! I read in a magazine that it's not healthy to hold your farts in. It's much better to let one rip, no matter where you are. Anyway, surely being the father of the bride carries some perks."

"Why should I stop farting? You shouldn't try to keep them in. The way I look at it is, what you can't hold in your hand you can't hold."

"Did you know your grandma can do impressions of farmyard animals? Not only can she do the sounds, she does the smells, too."

"I meant to say don't put that in your mouth because it's a rectal thermometer. I'm sure it's fine though – it's been in the dishwasher."

"The doctors say it's a miracle I'm still alive. They said they've never known a case like it. They had to open me right up. Five-hour operation. The nurses said afterwards that there was blood and guts everywhere – it was just like an episode of *ER*. Would you like to see my scar? Oh, okay, after you've served the next customer."

"My thrombosis means I can hardly walk, my eczema's been playing me up something rotten, my blood pressure is in danger of going through the roof, I can't see out of my left eye, and my lumbago means I haven't slept properly for over three months. Still, mustn't grumble."

"When you get to my age, you know you're not going to able to stay healthy. So it's more a case of finding an illness you like."

"The only reason I wear glasses is for little things, like driving my car – or finding it."

"What do you mean, Mildred, your eyes aren't what they used to be? What did they used to be? Ears? Spring onions? Wellington boots?"

"I'll tell you the worst thing about undergoing a lung transplant – coughing up someone else's phlegm."

"The doctor says I mustn't lift anything heavier than ten pounds, so I have to ask your mother to hold my pecker while I pee."

"Wrinkle cream doesn't work. I've been using it for eighteen months and my balls still look like raisins."

"Here's a medical tip I picked up: never take a sleeping pill and a laxative on the same night."

"Home remedies. What a waste of time! They always say things like, 'If you're choking on an ice cube, pour a cup of boiling water down your throat and the blockage will be almost instantly removed!'"

"What do you mean, you don't snore? I had to roll you over in bed last night so that you didn't inhale the curtains."

"The dentist told your mother she grinds her teeth at night. So now before we go to sleep I fill her mouth with hot water and coffee beans and set the alarm for eight o'clock."

"Your mother's no spring chicken, although she has got as many chemicals in her as one."

"So you don't think a singing mammogram is a fun idea for your mother's sixty-fifth birthday?"

"Here's a game you can play, kids. See if you can make animal shapes by joining up the veins on your grandma's legs. I reckon there could be a good giraffe in there somewhere."

"What do you mean, what was it like to be in a coma? How the fuck should I know? I was in a coma."

"The new pacemaker's okay, doctor, except that every time I approach my house, the garage doors automatically open."

"Ill health? You don't know what ill health is. I've spent so much time in hospital over the past two years that I'd forgotten what it was like to be wearing clothes that open in the front."

"Health plans are a waste of money. They're like hospital gowns – you only think you're covered."

"What in tarnation do you want with health insurance, woman? They'll only cover you for diseases you haven't already had, so that only leaves hard pad, foot and mouth, myxomatosis and testicular cancer."

"Your mother's been on cloud nine since the doctor told her she had acute angina. We must get her hearing tested."

"Your mother's having her stomach stapled next week. I'm going to ask the doctor if he can do her tongue while he's at it."

"Your father's always had a lazy eye, but now it has started to spread to the rest of his body."

"I have to take so many tablets that I rattle when I walk."

"Your mother used to spend all her time reading cookery books, but now her head's always in the medical dictionary, trying to find out whether there's an ailment she hasn't yet had."

"I think it's fair to say that your mother enjoys ill health."

"Oh, that's wonderful news! George, did you hear that? They're thinking about naming a disease after me."

"You've got period pains? I'm sorry to hear that, honey, but why don't you tell your uterus to stop being such a pussy!"

"I know I'm very quiet tonight, sweetheart. That's because it's your grandpa's turn with the teeth."

"You don't go to the doctor just because you've got a bad cold. It'll sort itself in a day or two. Real men only go to the doctor if their nuts are dropping off or if half their dick has been sliced off by an electric chainsaw – and even then only if two paracetamol tablets don't ease the pain."

"You've had a few stitches, that's all, George. I don't think anybody's going to start calling you 'Scarface' on the strength of three stitches."

"It's a tiny splinter in your finger, George, nothing worse. I don't think you need to worry about gangrene setting in just yet."

"I know a rectal examination isn't very pleasant, George, but I'm sure the doctor will take his wedding ring off."

"I don't care whether you'll be wearing gloves, doc, there's no way you're giving me a rectal examination with finger nails that long."

"Of course I need to look at my handkerchief! There's no point poking it in your ear with your finger if you don't inspect it to see what you've got out!"

"How do I know what type of virus I've got? 'Virus' is just a Latin word used by doctors meaning 'your guess is as good as mine'."

"There must be something to this acupuncture business. I mean, you never see any sick porcupines."

"It's lovely to see you, too, sweetheart. But don't hug Grandma too tightly in case my colostomy bag bursts."

"Your father and I used to give blood regularly – not through any great sense of duty but it was the only way we could get a free cup of tea and a biscuit on a Tuesday afternoon."

"Why should I grow old gracefully? What's the point in that? I intend to have facelifts until my ears meet."

"You want to know my secret for a long and healthy life? I never touched a cigarette, a drink or a girl until I was eleven years old."

"Why would I want to exercise? If God wanted me to touch my toes, he would have put them on my knees."

"They're always going on about men in their sixties not exercising enough. If they want us to exercise more, all they have to do is make the TV remote heavier."

"If I want to get fit, I'll go for a walk – I don't need an exercise DVD by some fifth-rate celebrity. So what if that actress from *EastEnders* has gone from a size 16 to a size 8? With any luck she'll soon evaporate altogether."

"At my age, the only thing I care to exercise is caution."

"Jim Henderson is dead?! That's terrible news. I sent him a letter only this morning. That's the price of a second-class stamp I'll never get back."

"I ain't afraid of dying – it's how long they expect you to stay dead. That's a damn long time if you stop and think about it."

"I'm quite looking forward to dying. After the insurance company managed to wriggle out of paying for my broken vase, I'll be interested to see how they try to talk their way out of this one!"

"My only regret is that the Co-op no longer does savings

stamps. I reckon if I'd have been buried with Co-op Funerals, there would have been enough stamps for George to buy a new motor mower."

"I'm very partial to a good funeral. I look upon them as a rehearsal for when it's my turn. Even while you're tucking into their salmon and cucumber sandwiches, people are still too upset to ask who you are."

"It may be more practical but if you don't mind I'd prefer not to be buried on top of your grandfather. I never did like it on top."

"When your father dies I'm going to have him cremated and I'll put his ashes in an egg timer. It will be the most work he's ever done."

"Do I want to be buried or cremated? Oh, I don't know. Surprise me."

# 13

# Old Wives' Tales

*Operating on the fringes of witchcraft, old people – especially women – love to put the fear of God into the younger generation by warning them of the dire consequences that will befall them should they wear tight underpants or leave the house with wet hair. These superstitions, many of which have been handed down over the centuries, may stop short of recommending passing a child three times under the belly of a donkey to cure whooping cough or carrying a dead shrew in your pocket to ward off rheumatism, but they definitely come under the category of alternative medicine. Of course, some people claim that old wives' tales were originally based on truth before becoming twisted in the re-telling. But that's probably just an old wives' tale.*

"If you keep wiping your nose, it will make it bigger."

"If you walk in bare feet, you'll get worms."

"If you eat on the toilet, you're feeding the devil."

"If you pull out a grey hair, ten more will grow in its place."

"Don't go out with wet hair. You'll catch your death of cold."

"If you cross your eyes, they'll stay that way."

"Don't pull faces at the dinner table. If the wind changes, you'll stay like that."

"If you sneeze with your eyes open, they'll pop out."

"If you fall asleep with your hands above your head, you'll suffocate."

"Don't try on someone else's glasses or you'll go blind."

"If you sit on cold walls or doorsteps, you'll get piles."

"Don't tickle a baby's feet; it will give the child a stutter when he or she is old enough to talk."

"Don't walk on the cracks in the pavement or bears will come up and eat you."

"Don't buy a green car. Green cars are unlucky. If you buy a green car, you'll die in it."

"Don't ever phone me during a thunderstorm because it could make lightning strike my house."

"Don't sleep with your head under the pillow or the tooth fairy will kick your teeth out."

"If you keep taking long hot baths, it will reduce your sperm count and you'll never be a father."

"Wearing tight underwear makes you less fertile."

"Don't wear other people's headphones – you'll get hearing AIDS."

"If you drink too much coffee, it will stunt your growth."

"You take care while eating that apple. If you swallow an apple seed, an apple tree will grow in your stomach."

"If you drop the comb while combing your hair, disappointment will follow."

"Seeing an ambulance is extremely unlucky unless you pinch your nose or hold your breath until you see a black dog."

"It's bad luck to leave a house through a different door from the one by which you entered."

"Never leave your shoes upside down – it's bad luck."

"You should never cut your fingernails on a Friday or a Sunday – it will bring bad luck."

"If you get out of bed in the morning with your left foot first, you'll have bad luck all day."

"It's bad luck to close a pocket knife unless you were the one who opened it."

"When you are making a bed, don't do anything else until you have finished making it or you will experience misfortune."

"If you're about to set off on a journey and your shoelace comes undone, stay at home instead. If you go ahead with the journey, you'll have bad luck."

"If a clock which hasn't been working suddenly chimes, there will be a death in the family."

"If three people are photographed together, the one in the middle will die first."

"Dropping an umbrella on the floor means that there will be a murder in the house."

"Keep cats away from babies because they suck the breath out of a child."

"You shouldn't let your underwear show above your pants. You don't want to get pregnant, do you?"

"If you're visiting someone in hospital, don't take cut flowers or a potted plant – they'll suck all the oxygen out of the air and kill the patient."

"If someone sweeping a floor sweeps under your feet, you'll never get married."

"If a woman sees something ugly during pregnancy, she'll have an ugly baby."

"If a man wears tight underpants, he'll father a baby girl."

"If your face gets rounder during pregnancy, you're having a girl; if your face is long and narrow, it's a boy."

"If a pregnant woman picks up a key by the rounded end, she's going to have a boy. If she picks the key up by the narrow end, she's expecting a girl. If she picks the key up in the middle, it's twins."

"If you cut an apple in half and see how many seeds are inside, it will tell you how many children you're going to have."

"If you spill pepper, you'll have a big argument with a close friend."

"If you count the number of fish you've caught, you won't catch any more that day."

"If you swallow chewing gum, at best it will take seven years to digest and at worst it will wrap itself around your heart and kill you."

"If you accidentally drop a pair of scissors, it is a sign that your lover is being unfaithful to you."

"A swarm of bees settling on your roof is a sure sign that your house will burn down."

"If you say goodbye to a friend on a bridge, you'll never see that person again."

"If grandchildren don't go to bed when they're told to, the bogeyman will come and get them."

"Place a cork under your pillow at night to relieve cramp."

"A wish will come true if you make it while burning onions."

"If you pick up burnt matches, you'll come into money."

"Always wear gloves when handling computer disks in case you catch a virus."

"If you rub the grease from church bells into your body, it will cure shingles."

"If you want to grow big breasts, eat cabbage – and that applies to you, too, Jason."

"Carry an acorn with you at all times to ensure good luck and a long life."

"If you catch a falling leaf on the first day of autumn, you won't catch a cold all winter."

"If you eat the crusts on your bread, it will make your hair curly."

"If your right ear itches, someone is speaking well of you; if your left ear itches, someone is speaking ill of you."

"Weather forecasters make it up as they go along. I prefer the science my own grandma taught me: if you see paper blowing along the street, it's a sure sign of rain. And if, when it rains, bubbles start to form on top of the puddles, that means it's going to rain for three days. See, you don't get information like that on the TV."

"We can always tell when it's going to rain by the state of your grandpa's joints. If he's creaking like a rusty old door hinge, expect a downpour."

"A cow with its tail to the west makes the weather best, a cow with its tail to the east makes the weather least. At any rate that's what they say. If you ask me, it's a load of old crap."

# 14

# Giving It To Them Straight

*Straight talking – that's what you get from old people. No concessions to sensitivities, no beating around the bush, no namby-pamby social worker, touchy-feely stuff, just honest blunt speaking, taking the bull by the horns, calling a spade a spade and avoiding clichés like the plague.*

"You look like a slut. Your mother would be proud of you."

"You're dressed like a hooker! In fact, if I was looking for a hooker, I'd drive right past you and try to find a classier-looking one."

"Hey, honey, dressed like that you should be on the cover of a magazine. Something like *Crack Whore*."

"You ain't got enough clothes on to wad a shotgun."

"Are you really going out looking like that? Have you ever heard the phrase 'mutton dressed as lamb'? Well you ain't even that good – you're mutton dressed as mutton."

"You look like ten pounds of shit in a nine-pound bag."

"So this is your new dress, but you say it looks much better on? On what? On fire?"

"That dress is about as sexy as socks on a rooster."

"You paid $300 for that dress? I wouldn't be seen dead in a ditch in it."

"Listen, honey, just because it was your size didn't mean you had to buy it."

"Oh, you've got a new coat, sweetheart. It's like the ones horses wear."

"That's not a hat, girl – it's an offensive weapon. You could have somebody's eye out with that hat!"

"Son, do you really think any girl is going to give you a second glance while you're wearing those clothes? I've seen better-dressed wounds."

"That's an interesting shirt. What brand is it? Clearance?"

"What do you look like, boy? Long hair, head band, beads and sandals – you're more like a bloody girl. Next thing, you'll be squatting to piss!"

"That side-parting makes you look like Hitler."

"I love your long hair, sweetie. It shines like shit on a barn door."

"You know, Rachel, your hair glistens in the rain much like a nose hair after a sneeze."

"Honey, the next time you get married I really think you should wear your hair down."

"Like I'm going to take advice from you on what to do with my hair – someone who still wears a mullet in his forties and consequently looks like an ageing porn star! But you think I should have a comb-over? And how exactly is my appearance going to be improved by combing my eight remaining strands across my head to create an effect that from above will look like an egg in the grasp of a large spider?"

"Yes, I know what hair extensions are, honey. All the top models wear them. They're very fashionable and very expensive. I realize this may sound like a radical idea, but have you ever considered just letting your hair grow long instead?"

"What do you mean, your hair's got a life of its own? Has

it enrolled in photography classes in college? Did you catch it in the kitchen last night making an omelette? Is it seeing other hair behind your back? It hasn't got a life of its own at all. It's just a fucking mess."

"Honey, I don't know why you spend so much time tending to your eyebrows. Here's how much men care about your eyebrows: do you have two of them? Okay, we're done."

"Listen to your granny: you don't need a bra yet, sweetheart. You have the chest of an eleven-year-old boy."

"There's nothing wrong with having small boobs, Jessica. At least you know they won't smack you in the face while you're running for the bus."

"You courtin' yet? . . . No? I'm not surprised. You ain't got very big tits. When I was your age I had tits you could lose an army in."

"Don't be self-conscious, sweetheart. I'm sure you'll eventually grow into your nose."

"I'm afraid noses run in the family, if you know what I mean. When your grandpa was young, his nose was so big he needed an axe to pick it."

"Just pray you never get a nose bleed, honey, or the room could look like the Red Sea."

"I'm not going to sit around while my granddaughter gets bullied at school. So come on, tell me which kid said you'd got a big nose, Pinoc . . . er, Penelope."

"Sorry, dear, I keep forgetting about the size of your nose. I thought you were eating a banana."

"Don't feel self-conscious, darling. I was just as pig ugly when I was your age."

"Good looks are a curse, sweetheart. You should count yourself lucky."

"You've had plastic surgery? Well, I'm pleased to see you obviously didn't pay much for it."

"Where the fuck did you get cosmetic surgery that left you looking like that? Through a mail-order catalogue?"

"Why have you spent all that money on facelifts when your neck's still got more wrinkles than an elephant's scrotum? You spent $10,000 on your face, why don't you spend 15 bucks on a fucking turtleneck?"

"Your aunt's like a lizard woman. She's had so many facelifts she pees through her ears, but all the cosmetic surgery in the world doesn't stop her looking like a Komodo dragon with Chanel accessories."

"I don't wish to appear critical, sweetheart, but there's a very thin line between a beauty spot and an unsightly blemish. I'm afraid yours is definitely veering toward the wart."

"Okay, so you're no oil painting, but look at the positives: not every woman is blessed with good elbows."

"Is that a beard, or are you eating a muskrat?"

"Are you deliberately growing a beard or is it just that you can't be arsed to shave?"

"You know, son, I'd have preferred you to have been gay than ginger."

"Just because you're crazy about Brigitte Bardot, was it wise to have the letter 'B' tattooed on both cheeks of your arse? You realize that every time you bend over naked, people will think you're in love with some guy called Bob?"

"And you don't think your prospects of a managerial post

at the bank will be harmed by that skull and crossbones tattoo on your neck?"

"Don't get any more tattoos – your body isn't a billboard."

"What's with the navel ring? There's only one thing should be in your belly button and that's fluff – lots of it."

"Why would you willingly want to put metal in your mouth? The only metal in my mouth is the fillings I had done on my back teeth when I was eight. See . . . these ones here."

"Don't even think about getting a nose stud or having your tongue pierced. You were born with the correct number of holes in your body. Don't make any more."

"What were you thinking about getting a tongue ring? Do you know what will happen if you poke your tongue out during a thunderstorm and lightning strikes it? Your tongue will fall off. You must be crazy!"

"Honey, if I ever find out that any granddaughter of mine has had a tattoo, I'll kill myself. And you'll have to live the rest of your life with that on your conscience."

"You hardly ever call me these days and, you know, Granny's not getting any younger. So if you do ever manage to fit in a visit, I'd like you to choose a few things you'd particularly like. Then when I'm gone, you can have them, and hopefully they'll be something to remember me by."

"I'm not guilt-tripping you. All I'm saying is I'm seventy-eight years old and therefore technically speaking I could die anytime. So next time you head off into town for two hours enjoying yourself with your friends, don't be surprised if you return home to find a corpse."

"I'm not trying to put pressure on you, sweetheart, but I would like grandchildren within the next couple of years before I'm too old and infirm to be able to appreciate them."

"Don't clip your nails so short, sweetheart. How else are

they supposed to find your killer's DNA if you are murdered?"

"Your grandma says your new boyfriend isn't conventionally handsome. What she means is, his dog probably closes its eyes while it humps his leg."

"Look at the state of her! She needs a good meal inside her. In fact, that's not all she needs inside her. Why, if I was fifty years younger and didn't have erectile dysfunction, I'd . . ."

"Maybe you could do with putting on a little weight, honey, because let's be honest, when you stick your tongue out you look like a zipper."

"Don't worry about putting on a little weight. As long as your belly doesn't stick out more than your boobs, you're okay."

"You're getting fat, honey. You need to work out. Same

goes for your boyfriend. Both of you are like turkeys waiting to be cooked."

"You could wear your mother's wedding dress – that would save us some money. But wait, you're a hell of a lot fatter than her."

"Maybe I shouldn't say this, sweetheart, but if you were to lose 12 pounds, you could make a killing in porn."

"I didn't say you were fat – all I said was I wouldn't get in an elevator with you unless I wanted to go down."

"You were so fat as a child, none of your friends would get on a see-saw with you. In fact, with you at one end it wasn't so much a see-saw at all – more like a catapult."

"Puppy fat? I've seen less puppy fat in *101 Dalmatians*."

"You've got a pretty big butt, sweetheart. You need to be

careful or when you get older it will be dragging along on the ground behind you."

"Your butt's too big for you to wear a skirt that tight. It looks like two pigs in a sack fighting for an ear of corn."

"I think you may have lost some weight, honey. Your double chin looks a little smaller to me."

"Unless you lose a little weight, sweetheart, anyone who wants to sweep you off your feet is going to need a hydraulic crane."

"Slim? Sure you look slim. Next to Orca the killer whale you look slim."

"Hey, is the ground getting higher or is your butt getting lower?"

"So you think you must be anorexic because whenever you

look in a mirror you see a fat person? No, honey, that's because you *are* fat."

"She's so fat it takes two dogs to bark at her."

"I prefer to use the term 'big boned'. I find it lends a certain dignity to chronic obesity. Remember the wrestler Giant Haystacks? He was big boned."

"She says she's approaching forty – but she doesn't say from which direction."

"You're starting to show your age in certain areas, George. This morning I found a dozen white pubic hairs on the toilet seat – it looked as if a polar bear had dropped by to do a shit."

"Have you seen that woman's skin? Her face looks like thirty miles of bad road."

"Why don't you try putting on a bit more makeup, darling? It's amazing what a little paint can do for an old barn."

"I just hope you age better than your mother. She's got enough crow's feet to start a bird sanctuary."

"You're going to have to stop lying about your age, Mildred, or soon you'll be younger than your daughter."

"Don't worry about your grandma's liver spots. She's hoping to join them up to make a tan."

"Sure your grandma dresses well, but it hides a multitude of sins. What you don't know is that beneath that designer frock she's got an arse like an accordion."

"Grandma can't wear sleeveless shirts any more because of the bingo wings around her upper arms. She'd look like a flying squirrel in drag."

"Your mother's been in that beautician's for three hours – and that's just for the estimate."

"Before I met your father, I'd never fallen in love. Mind you, I'd stepped in it a few times."

"Your grandma doesn't need to shave her legs as much these days because when you reach a certain age that kind of growth slows down. The other good thing is that it gives her more time to tend to the moustache that's started growing on her top lip."

"George, isn't it time you did something about all that ear-hair? It looks like the Enchanted Forest in there."

"Don't worry about your grandma. She's just upset that she's missed out on the Rear of the Year title yet again."

"Even at eighty-three, your grandpa's got a mind like a steel trap – unfortunately one that has been left outside so long, it has rusted shut."

"You don't think your mother looks sixty-eight? That's kind of you to say so, but I'll tell you something, son: a woman is as old as she looks before breakfast."

"One of the first things I remember about your mother was that she had a deep, throaty, genuine laugh, like that sound a dog makes just before it throws up."

"What do you mean, I don't express my emotions? I told you I loved you forty years ago, and if anything changes, I'll let you know."

"What is it with women and shoes? You ask them why they need yet another pair, and they say: 'In case I go somewhere different.' You're eighty-three years old, woman, where are you likely to be going that's different at your time of life? The moon? Sure, I can just hear the head of NASA saying: 'I know who we need for our next space mission – an old woman with a dodgy hip, arthritic joints and a weak bladder.'"

"Here's a joke for you, son. Why did your mother cross the road? – To get to the first shoe shop we went in two and a half fucking hours ago."

"What am I doing? I'm darning one of your old socks. Why, what did you think I was doing – making a pair of pants for a fish?"

"I would never divorce your father. I'd just bludgeon him to death with an axe and bury him in the backyard."

"You and your sister inherited your big boobs from your father."

"No, sweetheart, Granddad isn't turning into a woman. They're his man boobs."

"Yes, Granddad's trousers do look a bit odd. But it's the fashion among older men to wear them up to their armpits . . . And the yellow stains down the front? Er, why don't we do a nice jigsaw puzzle?"

"Well, I'm not sorry his house has been repossessed. Enjoying the misfortunes of others is the only pleasure some of us get at our time of life."

"You are what you eat? Whose shit idea is that? Is that why you have the mentality of a vegetable?"

"Vegetables are for rabbits and Seventh Day Adventists."

"Just because you're a vegetarian doesn't mean I have to be one, too. Of course I'll respect your beliefs but frankly I didn't climb to the top of the food chain to eat fucking lettuce!"

"I appreciate that you're a vegetarian and that therefore your dietary needs are different from mine, but you're not really going to eat that shit, are you?"

"You can't tell me a vegetarian diet is good for you when it makes you fart like that, George."

"I think you should take some cooking lessons, honey. That chicken dish was so bad I had to lick the cat's ass to get the taste out of my mouth."

"I'll give you nouvelle bloody cuisine! I've seen more meat on my wife's dentures. We've paid good money to eat in this restaurant, so the least I expect is a piece of steak that looks as if it could stand up for itself in a fight with a sprig of parsley."

"What sort of carvery is this? One slice of fucking pork? Do I look like a supermodel to you, pal?"

"Hey, waiter, if I'd known the service was going to be this slow I'd have brought my sleeping bag."

"No way am I eating with chopsticks! I want to eat with recognizable cutlery, not a pair of knitting needles. The object is to get the food into my mouth, not all over the tablecloth."

"Oh, you can eat with chopsticks, can you, son? Well, bully for you! But don't get too carried away with your achievement. It's not like you've discovered a cure for world poverty."

"I don't care if it's mayo or Miracle Whip. Just put it on my fucking sandwich."

"I'm not eating any of that curry muck. It looks like a plate of diarrhoea."

"Oxtail soup? No thank you, dear. What makes you think I would want to eat something that has spent its life swatting flies from a cow's arse?"

"I see your favourite fish is on the menu, Mildred. You haven't had red snapper since the time you forgot to put on sun cream during that holiday in Greece."

"How should I know if the yoghurt's safe to eat? Have you

tried looking at the date on the pot? Alternatively, if I find you dead in your bed in the morning, I'll hazard a guess that the answer was probably 'no'."

"Latte? What's a latte? I just want an ordinary coffee. I don't care what you call it. Anyway isn't latte just Latin for 'you paid too much for that coffee'?"

"No, I don't want milk in my coffee. I take my coffee the same way I take my women – black and bitter."

"Give me that pickle jar, son. You've got hands like your mother. You'll never open it."

"That's not what I call drunk. In my book you're not drunk if you can lie on the floor without holding on."

"Why the hell would I want water with my Scotch? I'm thirsty, not dirty."

"No, I'd better not have any champagne, dear. Champagne makes me fart."

"You're off back-packing in Colombia, son, but you don't think it will be too dangerous because you're used to roughing it outdoors? You mean when you were eighteen you once pitched a tent at the end of the garden – and even then you came back into the house when it started to rain."

"At your age you should be out playing sport, not sitting at home watching it on TV. You don't think Roger Federer got to be world number one by lounging on the sofa with a six-pack and a pizza."

"All sports are great. Well, except for rhythmic gymnastics. Since when has running around with a ribbon qualified as a sport? And I only watch ice skating in the hope that one of the competitors will fall through the ice. And darts is just a pub game – you can't play it unless you're half pissed. And stuff like judo and taekwondo leaves me cold. Why don't they just hammer the shit out of each other? As for synchronized swimming, it's fine if it's performed by dolphins at Marine World. Otherwise forget it. But yeah, I love sport."

"Son, I can see straight away what's wrong with your golf game: you stand too close to the ball – after you've hit it."

"How good do I think you are at golf? I'd say you were probably a 27 handicap, but you could easily be mistaken for a 28."

"Is my friend in the bunker or is the bastard on the green?"

"You can delude yourself all you want, but going to church does not make you a Christian any more than standing in a garage makes you a car."

"Sure you can borrow my car, son. But if it comes to a situation between you and the car, save the car. I can replace you."

"Son, why do you have to give your car a stupid name, like Mabel? It's not going to stop it breaking down, just because you try to humanize it. In fact, looking at this heap of rust you'd be better off calling it Flattery, because it will get you nowhere!"

"There's not much legroom in this car? You can say that again! I've been in bigger women!"

"Boy, where did you learn to drive? On bumper cars at the fair?"

"Yeah, that's fine, son, you park here. No problem. I can walk the rest of the way to the kerb."

"I hate to shatter your illusions of stardom, darling, but your singing sounds worse than a stray cat in a fan belt."

"Sorry, honey, but you couldn't carry a tune in a bucket."

"Sure, the tune you played was catchy. But so was the bubonic plague."

"Don't listen to your father. The only note he can hold has got the Queen's head on it."

"That's supposed to be a drawing of Grandma, is it? Well at least we'll know not to waste money on buying you crayons in future."

"All I'm saying is look on the box and see the amazing models other kids can make out of Plasticine – things like elephants, people, forests, castles. Really impressive, imaginative stuff. Two hours he's been playing with it, and the best he has managed is a draught excluder for a doll's house. Doesn't that tell you something?"

"Son, I don't want to sound unkind but, in the immortal words of Edmund Blackadder, you ride a horse rather less well than another horse would."

"You're not joking when you say you've got two left feet. The dog's got two left feet but even he can dance better than you!"

"Must you walk around the house half naked, Alison? I don't want the dog getting ideas."

"I don't like dogs and I don't like cats. Dogs lick their asses, then try to lick your face. That's nasty as hell! Cats are too damn independent – they're assholes."

"I didn't say your new girlfriend was a dog! All I said was, 'Will she be sleeping in the spare room or the kennel?'"

"Lady Gaga is a woman? Who says? She's got more balls than the US Open tennis tournament."

"You say Lady Gaga has a stalker? I bet she has one every morning when she wakes up."

"Do we have to watch a chick-flick? I swear if I sit through another one I'll start growing tits!"

"What's the big deal with this Justin Bieber? He just looks

like an ordinary kid to me. As a matter of fact, he's a bit on the geeky side. Hell, that could have been me sixty years ago! But no girls ever screamed at me – except for the time I mooned at their school bus."

"I'll say one good thing for that Simon Cowell: when he flashes those teeth we save on our electricity bill."

"Oi, Cowell, put a sandwich on the bottom of your shoe and invite your trousers down for dinner."

"You sure this shit is called rap music? They didn't miss off the 'c'?"

"Look at Andrew Lloyd Webber. Clever man. Extremely talented. But be honest, only a mother could love a face like that."

"I think people go to see The Rolling Stones in concert for the same reason they watch Nascar; if they go around enough times, maybe someone will die."

"Doesn't that Bruce Springsteen guy you're so fond of play any other type of music? Doesn't he know any nice country and western songs?"

"You reckon Obamaman needs more time? JFK got ten times more shit done on a weekend – and he was Catholic."

"If any airport security staff try body-searching me, they'll get more than they bargained for, I can tell you. At the very least I'll let a cabbagey one go in their face."

"When I said it should be a family occasion, I meant close family – not cousins. Cousins don't count – they're not proper family. I don't do cousins."

"Of course we were sorry when you eventually left home, honey – although we had been waiting. For years, your father left a ladder outside your bedroom window, but still you didn't take the hint."

"Of course you should have a curfew for your prom, dear.

I remember your mother stayed out very late at her senior prom and I ended up having to take her to visit that so-called doctor round the back of the coach station."

"I don't know why you're so shocked at seeing me naked after all this time. After all, it's where you came from."

"Where were you conceived? What kind of a question is that? If you must know, you were conceived in a pub toilet. That's why we called you Lou."

"Your sister was planned, but with you, I got horribly drunk on a night out and when I got home your father took advantage of me. That's why I haven't touched alcohol since."

"Honey, your brother is living proof that the diaphragm does not work."

"I'm not saying you weren't wanted, darling. It's more like you were an uninvited guest at a party."

"You weren't born naturally, you were Caesarean. You were surgically removed – like a tumour."

"How's that father of yours, boy? Is he still a wanker?"

"You're a special needs teacher, are you? So you teach simple kids?"

"Come on, it's an American tradition, like fathers chasing their kids around with power tools."

"You see far too many shoulders on TV these days. Wherever you look, there are women showing their naked shoulders. It's not right. And they'll catch their death of cold."

"I'll tell you what I think is wrong: breastfeeding in public. The baby's head obscures your view."

"Breastfeeding should be done discreetly, but some mothers

just whip their boobs out in the most public places. I may sound old fashioned but I don't think it's particularly nice to see. I mean, if I need the toilet, I don't pull my pants down in the middle of a café and have a shit."

"That baby's crying because it's hungry. And it doesn't want feeding from a bottle either. If you ask me, what it needs is a good tit."

"When you're flying on a plane I reckon all crying babies should be stored in the overhead compartment."

"I know you haven't knitted for years, Mildred, but I'm sure Jane appreciates your efforts. Anyway you never know, it might be fine – the baby might be born with only one arm."

"What do you mean, isn't he a beautiful baby? No, he's not, because babies aren't beautiful. They all look like Churchill."

"You reckon he's the spitting image of you, son? No, he's the spitting image of a bulldog in a romper suit."

"Whoever said all babies are cute never saw you as a child, son."

"Jonathan, as your mother it pains me to say it, but you were such an ugly baby that your incubator had tinted windows."

"Ah yes, look, he's got his grandma's eyes. Stop playing with them and give them back to her, will you – she can't see a thing without them."

"Your cousin Peter's family came to visit last week and brought their three year old. They said he's really clever and way ahead of all the other kids at play group. Yet when I tried to engage him in a meaningful discussion about Pythagoras' theorem he just looked at me blankly. I'm telling you, the kid's overrated."

"Yes, it's great that he can play the recorder at six – albeit badly. That doesn't mean you've got a child prodigy on your hands. He needs to learn a bit more – maybe a second note – before you can promote him as the next fucking Mozart."

"So the baby's only three months old but already he's responding to sounds? Hold the front page! You'd respond to sounds if someone kept shaking a rattle in your face every couple of minutes. The kid's probably already a nervous wreck and will need counselling by the time he's five."

"He's a baby. He does what babies do – shit and puke. Anything else is a bonus."

"I don't care if he is my grandson – if he dribbles milk down the front of my suit at the christening, I'll be sending him the cleaning bill. He needs to learn to hold his drink at an early age."

"If you drive up to my house, park in the driveway and

honk the horn, you better be delivering a pizza because you won't be taking my daughter out."

"I know you're only sixteen, but you can still have a beer with me, boy. You'll need one if you're planning on fucking my granddaughter."

"Remember that you're dating my granddaughter. Break her heart and I can make your death look like an accident."

"If your father catches you kissing like that, you'd better hope that your boyfriend can drive fast and has bullet-proof windows."

"I don't know why you let that boyfriend of yours mess you about the way he does. He's always seeing other girls behind your back. If that were me, I'd cut off his whatnots with a pair of garden shears – the rustier the better."

"Sweetheart, I hope you aren't going to marry one of those weird boys with holes in their ears."

"Why have you got a picture of that boy band singer on your bedroom wall, honey? He's gay, ain't he? You'd be better off aiming all those teenage hormones at someone who appreciates what you have to offer rather than some shirt-lifter."

"Alex, I'm sure your fiancée would love to see what you looked like when you were a boy. I just happen to have the album right here. Look, Kate, this is Alex when he was two. Ugly little fucker, wasn't he?"

"It doesn't seem possible that you're forty-one now. I can still remember what you were like as a baby as if it were yesterday. I was only just saying to your fiancée, no child could fill a nappy like our Michael."

"What happened to that girl you brought home the other week – the one with the bad breath and fat thighs? Oh, sorry, dear, I didn't recognize you."

"What happened to that young man you went out with last week, darling – the one your grandad said looked like a rapist?"

"Nice to meet you, Daniel. What a gentle handshake. Tell me, are you one of those? Do you bat for the other side?"

"So you're Philip's wife? Nice to meet you at last. You're not as frumpy as I imagined."

"You must be Jenny. We've heard so much about you. Don't take this the wrong way, dear, but you look much better in photographs."

"Good to meet you, Chelsea. Nice breasts. My compliments to your surgeon."

"So this is your new boyfriend? Pleased to meet you, Ben. Tell me, Miranda, is he a good lover?"

"Why haven't you ever brought your new boyfriend to see me? There's nothing wrong with him, I hope. He's not Welsh, is he?"

"So this is the young man you're going to marry? I guess he'll make a good first husband."

"So this is the lovely young lady that you're planning to spend the rest of your life with? I'll give it six months."

# 15

# The Thoughts of Famous Wrinklies

"Look at it this way: if we all ate one person, the problem would be halved overnight. Think about it: I could eat someone you don't like, you could eat someone I don't like. Where's the fucking damage?" Billy Connolly

"I think it would be interesting if old people got anti-Alzheimer's disease where they slowly began to recover other people's lost memories." George Carlin

"Whenever I'm confused, I just check my underwear. It holds the answer to all the important questions." Grampa Simpson, *The Simpsons*

"Apparently women need to feel loved to have sex and men need to have sex to feel loved, so the basic act of continuing the species requires a lie from one of you." Billy Connolly

"My ninety-three-year-old neighbour calls his manhood Carpool Lane, because he knows it's there, but he can't use it." George Miller

"The human male is physically capable of enjoying sex up to and even beyond the age of eighty. Not as a participant of course . . ." Denis Norden

"Now that I'm seventy-eight, I do tantric sex because it's very slow. My favourite position is called the plumber. You stay in all day but nobody comes." John Mortimer

"I only take Viagra when I'm with more than one woman." Jack Nicholson

"Don't have sex. It leads to kissing and pretty soon you

have to start talking to them." Steve Martin

"Sex without love is an empty experience, but as empty experiences go, it's one of the best." Woody Allen

"A man can sleep around, no questions asked, but if a woman makes nineteen or twenty mistakes she's a tramp." Joan Rivers

"When a man talks dirty to a woman, it's sexual harassment. When a woman talks dirty to a man, it's five dollars a minute." Steven Wright

"My husband complained to me. He said, 'I can't remember when we last had sex.' And I said, 'Well I can and that's why we ain't doin' it.'" Roseanne Barr

"If God had intended us not to masturbate, he would have made our arms shorter." George Carlin

"If God had meant us to walk around naked, he would never have invented the wicker chair." Erma Bombeck

"My sex life is now reduced to fan letters from an elderly lesbian who wants to borrow $800." Groucho Marx

"My body is falling so fast my gynaecologist wears a hard hat." Joan Rivers

"If you can't remember the last time you had sex with a woman, you're either gay or married." Jeff Foxworthy

"Everything that goes up must come down. But there comes a time when not everything that's down can come up." George Burns

"At my age, getting a little action means the prune juice is working." George Burns

"My pubic hair is going grey. In a certain light you'd swear it was Stewart Granger down there." Billy Connolly

"The simple truth is that balding African-American men look cool when they shave their heads whereas balding white men look like giant thumbs." Dave Barry

"I don't need you to remind me of my age, I have a bladder to do that for me." Stephen Fry

"I don't want to live to be a hundred. I don't think I could stand to see bell-bottom pants three times." Jeff Foxworthy

"When you get old, first you forget names, then you forget faces. Next you forget to pull your zipper up and finally you forget to pull it down." George Burns

"When you become senile, you won't know it." Bill Cosby

"By the time you're eighty years old, you've learned everything. You only have to remember it." George Burns

"I'm at the age when my back goes out more than I do."
Phyllis Diller

"Like everyone else who makes the mistake of getting older,
I begin each day with coffee and obituaries." Bill Cosby

"As you get older, never pass up a bathroom, never waste
a hard-on, and never trust a fart." Jack Nicholson

"As you grow old, you lose interest in sex, your friends drift
away and your children often ignore you. There are other
advantages, of course, but these are the outstanding ones."
Richard Needham

"You know you're getting old when, by the time you've lit
the last candle on your cake, the first one has burned out."
Jeff Rovin

"I was introduced to a beautiful young lady as a gentleman
in his nineties. Early nineties, I insisted." George Burns

"When a man has a birthday, he takes a day off. When a woman has a birthday, she takes three years off." Joan Rivers

"I have my eighty-seventh birthday coming up and people ask me what I'd most appreciate getting. I'll tell you – a paternity suit." George Burns

"Dress simply. If you wear a dinner jacket, don't wear anything else on it – like lunch or dinner." George Burns

"I used to be with it, then they changed what *it* was. Now what I'm with isn't it and what's it seems weird and scary. It'll happen to yooouuu." Grampa Simpson, *The Simpsons*

"At a formal dinner party, the person nearest death should always be seated closest to the bathroom." George Carlin

"There are worse things in life than death. If you've ever spent an evening with an insurance salesman, you know what I'm talking about." Woody Allen

"The only two times they pronounce you anything in life are when they pronounce you 'man and wife' or 'dead on arrival'." Dennis Miller

"I don't want to achieve immortality through my work. I want to achieve it through not dying." Woody Allen

"I'm always relieved when someone is delivering a eulogy and I realize I'm listening to it." George Carlin

"When I was growing up they used to say, 'Robin, drugs can kill you.' Now that I'm fifty-nine my doctor's telling me, 'Robin, you need drugs to live.' I realize now that my doctor is also my dealer." Robin Williams

"Now I'm getting older, I don't need to do drugs any more. I can get the same effect just by standing up real fast." Jonathan Katz

"You're fifty years old. Can they make a drug to help you through all of that, to keep all your organs intact until your golden years? No. Can they make a drug to give mental clarity to your golden time? No. What they've got is Viagra, a drug to make you harder than Chinese algebra." Robin Williams

"There are better things in life than alcohol, but it makes up for not having them." Terry Pratchett

"Don't smoke too much, drink too much, eat too much or work too much. We're all on the road to the grave, but there's no need to be in the passing lane." Robert Orben

"Getting out of hospital is like resigning from a book club. You're not out of it until the computer says you're out." Erma Bombeck

"My idea of exercise is a good brisk sit-down." Phyllis Diller

"I'm Jewish. I don't work out. If God had wanted us to bend over, he'd put diamonds on the floor." Joan Rivers

"A friend of mine runs marathons. He always talks about this 'runner's high'. But he has to go twenty-six miles for it. That's why I smoke and drink. I get the same feeling from a flight of stairs." Larry Miller

"I don't know how this word came into being – 'aerobics'. I guess gym instructors got together and said: 'If we're going to charge ten dollars an hour, we can't call it "jumping up and down"'." Rita Rudner

"Life expectancy would grow by leaps and bounds if green vegetables smelled as good as bacon." Doug Larson

"I would like to find a stew that will give me heartburn immediately instead of at three o'clock in the morning." John Barrymore

"Waiters and waitresses are becoming nicer and more caring. I used to pay my cheque and they would say: 'Thank you.' That's now escalated into: 'You take care of yourself.' The other day, I paid my cheque and the waiter said: 'Don't put off that mammogram.'" Rita Rudner

"Hell, when I was in high school, a 'drive-by shooting' meant somebody had their rear end hanging out a car window!" Jeff Foxworthy

"My husband gave me a necklace. It's fake. I requested fake. Maybe I'm paranoid but in this day and age, I don't want something around my neck that's worth more than my head." Rita Rudner

"If you can't beat them, arrange to have them beaten." George Carlin

"Build a man a fire and he'll be warm for a day. Set a man on fire and he'll be warm for the rest of his life." Terry Pratchett

"Always read stuff that will make you look good if you die in the middle of it." P.J. O'Rourke

"There are times not to flirt. When you're sick, when you're with children, when you're on the witness stand." Joyce Jillson

"Start every day off with a smile and get it over with."
W. C. Fields

"Let a smile be your umbrella and you'll end up with a faceful of rain." George Carlin

"Before you judge a man, walk a mile in his shoes. After that who cares? He's a mile away and you've got his shoes." Billy Connolly

"Find an aim in life before you run out of ammunition." Arnold H. Glasow

"If you can't dazzle them with brilliance, baffle them with bull." W. C. Fields

"Never lend your car to anyone to whom you have given birth." Erma Bombeck

"If you love someone, set them free; if they come home, set them on fire." George Carlin

"If you're going to do something tonight that you'll be sorry for tomorrow morning, sleep late." Henny Youngman

"Never pick a fight with an ugly person – they've got nothing to lose." Robin Williams

"Don't worry about the world coming to an end today. It's already tomorrow in Australia." Charles Schulz

"Honesty may be the best policy, but it's important to remember that apparently, by elimination, dishonesty is the second-best policy." George Carlin

"If at first you don't succeed, try, try again. Then quit. No use being a damn fool about it." W. C. Fields

"Family, Religion, Friendship. These are the three demons you must slay if you wish to succeed in business." Mr Burns, *The Simpsons*

"Getting information from the Internet is like trying to get a glass of water from Niagara Falls." Arthur C. Clarke

"You can email me, but I prefer letters that come through conventional mail. I like letters that have been licked by strangers." David Letterman

"I hate all those weathermen who tell you that rain is bad weather. There's no such thing as bad weather, just the wrong clothing." Billy Connolly

"They've gotta stop reporting wind chill. That's nonsense. It really is. I don't know where they came up with it, why they came up with it, but it's a lie. They come on: 'Well, it's 27 degrees today, but with the wind chill, it's minus 3.' Well, then it's minus 3, asshole! I don't need to know what the weather was like if the conditions were perfect!" Lewis Black

"It's absolutely stupid that we live without an ozone layer. We have men, we've got rockets, we've got saran wrap – fix it!" Lewis Black

"There are many mysteries in old age, but the greatest, surely, is this: in those adverts for walk-in bathtubs, why doesn't all the water gush out when you get in?" Alan Coren

"Somebody just gave me a shower radio. Thanks a lot. Do you really want music in the shower? I guess there's no better place to dance than a slick surface next to a glass door." Jerry Seinfeld

"I wonder sometimes if manufacturers of foolproof items keep a fool or two on their payroll to test things." Alan Coren

"Why do people use phrases like 'happens to be', like in 'he happens to be black'? Like it's a fucking accident, you know. He had two black parents? Yes, that's right, two black parents. And they fucked? Oh, indeed they did. So where does the surprise part come in? I would think it would be more unusual if he just 'happened to be' Scandinavian." George Carlin

"Why do the medical profession still keep writing on prescription bottles in a size that only a twenty year old can read? You were standing there with the medicine bottle in your hand and you died because you couldn't read the directions!" Bill Cosby

"On life's list of fun things to do, visiting my in-laws comes in somewhere below sitting in a tub full of scissors." Jeff Foxworthy

"Some day I want to be rich. Some people get so rich they lose all respect for humanity. That's how rich I want to be." Rita Rudner

"A bank is a place that will lend you money if you can prove that you don't need it." Bob Hope

"What good is money if you can't inspire terror into your fellow man?" Mr Burns, *The Simpsons*

"Sometimes the road less travelled is less travelled for a reason." Jerry Seinfeld

"A good rule of thumb is if you've made it to thirty-five and your job still requires you to wear a name tag, you've probably made a serious vocational error." Dennis Miller

"I don't like young guys. I'm always scared I'll wake up and think: 'Is this my date or did I give birth last night?'" Joan Rivers

"After you've dated someone, it should be legal to stamp them with what's wrong with them so the next person doesn't have to start from scratch." Rita Rudner

"Don't cook, don't clean. No man will ever make love to a woman because she waxed the linoleum. 'My God, the floor's immaculate. Lie down, you hot bitch!'" Joan Rivers

"Trust your husband, adore your husband, and get as much as you can in your own name." Joan Rivers

"Think like a second wife. You grab and you take. You grab and you take. And when you die, whatever you got out of him you have buried on you. If the next bitch wants it, make her dig for it." Joan Rivers

"Marry an outdoors woman. Then if you throw her out into the yard on a cold night, she can still survive." W. C. Fields

"If you never want to see a man again, say 'I love you, I want to marry you, I want to have your children.' Sometimes they leave skid marks." Rita Rudner

"Your marriage is in trouble if your wife says, 'You're only interested in one thing,' and you can't remember what it is." Milton Berle

"Divorce comes from the Latin word *divorcerum* meaning

'to have your genitals torn out through your wallet'."
Robin Williams

"The difference between divorce and legal separation is that a legal separation gives a husband time to hide his money." Johnny Carson

"No doubt exists that all women are crazy; it's only a question of degree." W. C. Fields

"Choosing a woman is like choosing a car. We all want a Ferrari, sometimes want a pickup truck, and end up with a station wagon." Tim Allen

"A man without a woman is like a neck without a pain." W. C. Fields

"Don't buy one of those baby intercoms. Babies pretend to be dead. They're bastards, and they do it on purpose." Billy Connolly

"Grandchildren can be annoying. How many times can you go, 'And the cow goes moo and the pig goes oink?' It's like talking to a supermodel." Joan Rivers

"The thing that best defines a child is the total inability to absorb information from anything not plugged in." Bill Cosby

"When I ask how old your toddler is, I don't need to know in actual months – like twenty-seven months. 'He's two,' will do just fine. He's not a cheese – and I don't really care in the first place." Bill Maher

"My son has taken up meditation. At least it's better than sitting and doing nothing." Max Kauffman

"Adolescence is the stage between puberty and adultery." Denis Norden

"It's extraordinary. One day, you look at your phone bill and realize your child is a teenager." Milton Berle

"Telling a teenager the facts of life is like giving a fish a bath." Arnold H. Glasow

"You can't say civilization isn't advancing; in every war they kill you in a new way." Will Rogers

"If the world should blow itself up, the last audible voice would be that of an expert saying it can't be done." Peter Ustinov

"What if everything is an illusion and nothing exists? In that case, I definitely overpaid for my carpet." Woody Allen

"I believe that if life gives you lemons, you should make lemonade. And try to find somebody whose life has given them vodka, and have a party." Ron White

"Life is a waste of time. Time is a waste of life. Get wasted all the time and you'll have the time of your life." Billy Connolly

"Life is like a sewer. What you get out of it depends on what you put into it." Tom Lehrer

"In life, it's not who you know that's important, it's how your wife found out." Joey Adams

"I believe you should live each day as if it was your last, which is why I don't have any clean laundry, because who wants to wash clothes on the last day of their life?" Jack Handey

"The important thing, I think, is not to be bitter. If it turns out that there is a God, I don't think that he is evil. I think that the worst thing you could say is that he is, basically, an under-achiever." Woody Allen

"So I say live and let live. That's my motto. Live and let live. Anyone who can't go along with that, take him outside and shoot the motherfucker. It's a simple philosophy, but it's always worked in our family." George Carlin

"Dear Advertisers, I am disgusted with the way old people are depicted on television. We are not all vibrant, fun-loving sex maniacs. Many of us are bitter, resentful individuals who remember the good old days when entertainment was bland and inoffensive. The following is a list of words I never want to hear on television again. Number one: bra. Number two: horny. Number three: family jewels." Grampa Simpson, *The Simpsons*

"I am free of all prejudices. I hate everyone equally." W. C. Fields

"I don't have pet peeves. I have major psychotic fucking hatreds! And it makes the world a lot easier to sort out." George Carlin